EARLIER AMERICAN MUSIC

EDITED BY H. WILEY HITCHCOCK
for the *Music Library Association*

15

THE BOSTON HANDEL AND HAYDN SOCIETY COLLECTION OF CHURCH MUSIC

THE BOSTON HANDEL
AND HAYDN SOCIETY COLLECTION
OF CHURCH MUSIC

Being a Selection of the Most Approved Psalm and Hymn Tunes

Together with Many Beautiful Extracts from the Works
of Haydn, Mozart, Beethoven, and Other Eminent Modern
Composers

Calculated for Public Worship or Private Devotion

COMPILED BY LOWELL MASON

NEW INTRODUCTION BY H. WILEY HITCHCOCK
Director, Institute for Studies in American Music,
Brooklyn College, CUNY

DA CAPO PRESS · NEW YORK · 1973

The Da Capo Press edition of *The Boston Handel and
Haydn Society Collection of Church Music* is an
unabridged republication of the first edition
published in Boston in 1822.

Library of Congress Catalog Card Number 77-171078

ISBN 0-306-77315-5

Copyright © 1973 by the Music Library Association

Published by Da Capo Press, Inc.
A Subsidiary of Plenum Publishing Corporation
227 West 17th Street, New York, N.Y. 10011

Manufactured in the United States of America

EDITOR'S FOREWORD

American musical culture, from Colonial and Federal Era days on, has been reflected in an astonishing production of printed music of all kinds: by 1820, for instance, more than fifteen thousand musical publications had issued from American presses. Fads, fashions, and tastes have changed so rapidly in our history, however, that comparatively little earlier American music has remained in print. On the other hand, the past few decades have seen an explosion of interest in earlier American culture, including earlier American music. College and university courses in American civilization and American music have proliferated; recording companies have found a surprising response to earlier American composers and their music; a wave of interest in folk and popular music of past eras has opened up byways of musical experience unimagined only a short time ago.

It seems an opportune moment, therefore, to make available for study and enjoyment and as an aid to furthering performance of earlier American music—works of significance that exist today only in a few scattered copies of publications long out of print, and works that may be well known only in later editions or arrangements having little relationship to the original compositions.

Earlier American Music is planned around several types of musical scores to be reprinted from early editions of the eighteenth, nineteenth, and early twentieth centuries. The categories are as follows:

> Songs and other solo vocal music
> Choral music and part-songs
> Solo keyboard music
> Chamber music
> Orchestral music and concertos
> Dance music and marches for band
> Theater music

The idea of *Earlier American Music* originated in a paper read before the Music Library Association in February, 1968, and published under the title "A Monumenta Americana?" in the Association's journal, *Notes* (September, 1968). It seems most appropriate, therefore, for the Music Library Association to sponsor this series. We hope *Earlier American Music* will stimulate further study and performance of Musical Americana.

H. Wiley Hitchcock

INTRODUCTION

The present volume contains very little American music. Yet it would be hard to overestimate its influence, and that of its compiler, on the course of nineteenth-century music in America.

The Boston Handel and Haydn Society Collection of Church Music was compiled by Lowell Mason, although his name does not appear on the original title page—at the time, he preferred not to be mistaken for a professional musician. It was the first of many such collections Mason got up. Together with these other, later books of hymns and anthems, Sunday-school music for children, and secular songs, plus his writings about music, his introduction of music into the curriculum of public schools, and his organizing of music-teacher training institutes, *The Boston Handel and Haydn Society Collection of Church Music* made Mason the single most influential figure in all of nineteenth-century American music. The impact of his taste and ideals, strengthened and diffused by a large circle of associates that included Thomas Hastings, George J. Webb, David Greene, W.B. Bradbury, and T.F. Seward, is incalculable. It decisively deflected American music from a British-based native tradition towards a "scientific" musical ideal rooted in the Classic-era masters of central Europe—Handel, Haydn, Mozart, and Beethoven; and in so doing, it helped to create a profound schism in American musical life between "popular" and "classical' music, between "vernacular" and "cultivated" traditions.

Lowell Mason was born in Medfield, Massachusetts, in 1792, into a musical family. At age thirteen he attended his first singing school under Amos Albee, compiler of *The Norfolk Collection of Sacred Harmony* (1805); he also had lessons with blind Oliver Shaw in nearby Dedham. While still in his teens, he directed the choir of the Medfield church and also the village band. Then, in 1812, Mason moved to Savannah, Georgia, where he went into business (dry goods), then into banking. But he continued to study music, especially after the German born Frederick L. Abel arrived in Savannah in 1817. That contact was crucial and, imbued with new musical ideals, Mason began compiling a collection of hymn tunes, arranged for three or four voices, under Abel's guidance. His main source of melodies was a big, multi-volume collection put together by the Englishman William Gardiner, *Sacred Melodies from Haydn, Mozart and Beethoven. Adapted to the English Poets. And Appropriated to the Use of The British Church* (1812 et seqq.); *its* sources are obvious from the title.

Mason's first collection was published as you see it here, after revision and approval by Boston's most esteemed musician (and mentor to the Handel and Haydn Society), Dr. George K. Jackson. It reflected perfectly the aims of the Society, those of "cultivating and improving a correct taste in the performance of sacred music, and also to introduce into more general practice the works of Handel, Haydn, and other eminent composers." With it, a new chapter in the history of American hymnody began.

H.W.H.

THE BOSTON HANDEL
AND HAYDN SOCIETY COLLECTION
OF CHURCH MUSIC

THE

BOSTON HANDEL AND HAYDN SOCIETY

COLLECTION OF CHURCH MUSIC;

BEING A SELECTION OF THE MOST APPROVED

PSALM AND HYMN TUNES;

TOGETHER WITH MANY BEAUTIFUL EXTRACTS FROM THE WORKS OF

HAYDN, MOZART, BEETHOVEN, AND OTHER EMINENT MODERN COMPOSERS.

NEVER BEFORE PUBLISHED IN THIS COUNTRY:

THE WHOLE HARMONIZED FOR THREE AND FOUR VOICES, WITH A FIGURED BASE FOR THE ORGAN OR PIANO FORTE.

CALCULATED FOR PUBLIC WORSHIP OR PRIVATE DEVOTION.

BOSTON:

PUBLISHED BY RICHARDSON AND LORD, NO. 75 CORNHILL.

....

PRINTED BY J. H. A. FROST, CONGRESS-STREET.

1822.

PREFACE.

THE HANDEL and HAYDN SOCIETY, having been instituted for the purpose of improving the style of Church Music, have felt it their duty to keep two objects continually in view ; the first to acquire and diffuse that style and taste in performance without which even the most exquisite compositions lose their effect and influence ; the second, what was indeed a necessary pre-requisite, to furnish the public with a selection of such compositions, both of ancient and modern authors, as are considered most excellent, and at the same time most useful.

With regard to the first of these objects, they reflect with great pleasure upon the success which has attended their efforts. A visible improvement has taken place in the style of singing, and consequently in the taste of the community. Not only the practice but the science and theory of music, have been the objects of great attention ; the increase of patronage has been commensurate with the increase of knowledge and fondness for the art : and the various collections of psalmody, and the number of editions to which some of them have passed, are sure and certain indications of increasing refinement in the public taste.

These favourable appearances have animated the exertions of the Society with regard to what they have mentioned as the second object of their attention ; and they have for some time been engaged with much labour, and at considerable expence, in collecting materials for the present work.

It is obvious that no collection of Sacred Music, can be so extensively useful in this country, as one of psalmody. The only question which can arise therefore, is with respect to the peculiar advantages to be derived from that which is now presented to the public.

The Handel and Haydn Society, have certainly no disposition to detract from the merits of the respectable collections which are now in use ; and they wish to avoid any appearance of depreciating the efforts of those whom they consider as fellow-labourers for the promotion of a common benefit. But, while they give that praise which is justly due to these laudable exertions, and acknowledge that much has been done, they are confident that all scientific and disinterested persons will agree with them that much still remains undone. Many respectable teachers of music in various parts of our country have frequently requested the Society to publish a new collection, and the advantages they enjoy for this purpose have seemed to them to render a compliance with this request an act of duty.

Their combination as a Society, and their local situation, have given them an extensive and easy access to the fountains of Music in Europe, and have enabled them to cultivate with advantage an intercourse with gentlemen of taste and science in our own country. As a Society also they are able to sustain an expence beyond the power of individual exertion; and by that division which is so necessary to the perfection of mental as well as bodily efforts, their labours have been rendered more effective.

While there has been in our country a great improvement in the taste for good melody, there has not been a correspondent attention to good harmony. To remedy this defect has been the special object of the Society in the present work.

Many of the oldest and best psalm tunes, as they were originally composed, were simple melodies; and as the practice of singing metre psalms in public worship was only allowed, not enjoined in England, and was confined to the parish churches, it was not much attended to by the principal masters, who were chiefly engaged in the composition of Cathedral Music. When therefore the other parts were added to these simple melodies, metre psalmody being considered of minor importance, the harmonies were mostly added by inferior composers. And even when the harmonies were original parts of the composition, a beautiful air might be composed without any of that science which was necessary to direct with propriety the inferior movements.

Of late years however a great change has taken place in the public sentiment with regard to the importance of psalmody, and this has of course called the attention of the most eminent masters in England to the subject. Several of them have been recently employed in harmonizing anew many of the old standard airs, and also in selecting and adapting movements from the works of Handel, Haydn, Mozart, Beethoven and other great masters, whose mighty talents have been displayed and acknowledged throughout Europe.

These works are among the materials to which the Handel and Haydn Society have had access, and they have exercised their best judgment in making such selections from them as would most enrich the present work. They consider themselves as peculiarly fortunate in having had, for the accomplishment of their purpose, the assistance of Mr. Lowell Mason, one of their members now resident in Savannah, whose taste and science have well fitted him for the employment, and whose zeal for the improvement of Church Music, has led him to undertake an important part of the labour in selecting, arranging and harmonizing the several compositions. But what has most contributed to the confidence with which they offer the present collection to the public, the whole work has been finally and most carefully revised by Doctor G. K. Jackson. The obligations which the Society owe to that gentleman for his gratuitous and unwearied labours, they have endeavoured in some measure to express, by prefixing his name to their work.

The Society are fully aware of the cautious delicacy with which variations should be admitted into tunes that by long use have become familiar, and by the power of association with holy purposes have been in some measure sanctified. They have been careful, therefore to retain in general, the airs of the several tunes unaltered; but as the longest usage cannot reconcile science and correct taste with false harmony, it has been found indispensably necessary to introduce changes into the accompanying parts. The leading part, however, being unaltered the change will not be such as to shock even the most accustomed ear; while the increased richness of the harmony cannot fail to increase the delight of every lover of Sacred Music.

It is obvious that these improvements will create an additional interest in psalmody, both in schools and societies, and in congregations for public worship. If the inferior parts are tame and spiritless, there will be a reluctance in the scholars or members of societies, to take them. The consequence must be that very unsuitable voices will sing upon the principal part, and thus materially injure the effect of the whole. The same remark is equally applicable to congregations for public worship. With regard to private worship, the improvements in harmony which have now been introduced will operate as an incitement to family devotion. Where there are three or more voices to be found in the same family, capable of sustaining the different parts, a much more powerful effect will be produced by a noble and expressive harmony, than if all should be confined to the Air alone.

The Society are far from thinking, that with all their care and advantages, they have produced a perfect work. Imperfection is the characteristic of every human effort; and works of this nature especially will approach the ideal standard, only by a slow and gradual approximation. They invite therefore the critical examination of all lovers of music, and scientific musicians, that even the most trivial errors may be rectified, and another edition, should another be called for, be rendered still more worthy of the public patronage.

To the *Trustees of the Boston Handel and Haydn Society.*

BOSTON, OCTOBER 5, 1821.

GENTLEMEN,

I have been highly gratified in the examination of the manuscript of the " HANDEL AND HAYDN SOCIETY COLLECTION OF CHURCH MUSIC." The selection of tunes is judicious—it contains all the old approved English melodies, that have long been in use in the church, together with many fine compositions from modern European authors. The whole are harmonized with great accuracy, taste and judgment, according to the acknowledged principles of musical science—while a simplicity has been observed which renders their performance easy. I consider the book as a valuable acquisition to the church, as well as to every lover of devotional music. It is much the best book of the kind I have seen published in this country, and I do not hesitate to give it my most decided approbation.

Very respectfully, Gentlemen,

Your obedient servant,

G. K. JACKSON.

HAVING critically examined the manuscript copy of " THE HANDEL AND HAYDN SOCIETY COLLECTION OF CHURCH MUSIC," I feel a pleasure in saying that the selection of tunes is not only judiciously made, but the parts are properly arranged—the Base is correctly figured, and in no instance are the laws of counterpoint and Thorough Base violated, as is the case in most American Musical Publications.

To all the lovers of sacred music, I cheerfully recommend it as a work in which taste, science and judgment are happily combined.

F. L. ABEL,

Professor of Music.

SAVANNAH.

THE HANDEL AND HAYDN SOCIETY

OF BOSTON,

DEDICATE

Their Collection of Church Music

TO

GEORGE K. JACKSON,

MUS. DOCT,

NOT ONLY

AS A TRIBUTE OF GRATITUDE,

FOR HIS GREAT CARE AND ATTENTION IN REVISING AND CORRECTING THEIR WORK ;

BUT ALSO

AS A TESTIMONY

OF THE HIGH ESTIMATION IN WHICH HE IS HELD

FOR HIS

EXQUISITE TASTE, PROFOUND KNOWLEDGE,

AND

UNRIVALLED SKILL,

IN THE

ART AND SCIENCE OF MUSIC.

Boston, October 12, 1821.

EXPLANATION OF MUSICAL TERMS.

A, signifies in, for, at, with, &c.

Adagio, (or *Ado*,) signifies the slowest time.

Ad libitum, as you please.

Affettuoso, tender and affecting.

Air, the leading part.

Allegretto, a little brisk.

Allegro, (or *Allo.*) brisk.

Alto, (or *Counter Tenor*,) that part which lies between the Treble and Tenor.

Amoroso, in a soft and delicate style.

Andante, rather slow and distinct.

Andantino, somewhat quicker than *Andante*.

Animated, with spirit and boldness.

Anthem, a composition for vocal music, the words of which are generally selected from the Psalms, and used in divine service.

Ardito, bold and energetic.

Assai, generally used with other words, to express an increase, or diminution of the time of any composition; as, *Adagio assai*, more slow; *Allegro assai*, more quick.

Base, the lowest part in a harmony.

Brilliante, signifies that the movement is to be performed in a gay, showy and sparkling style.

Canon, a vocal composition, in two or more parts, so constructed as to form a perpetual fugue.

Cantabile, in a graceful, elegant and melodious style.

Canto, (or *Cantus*,) the Treble.

Chorus, signifies that all the voices sing on their respective parts.

Con, with; as *con spirito*, with spirit.

Crescendo, (or *Cres.*) to increase the sound.

Da Capo, (or *D. C.*) to return and end with the first strain.

Diminuendo, to diminish the sound.

Dolce, sweet and soft.

Duo, (or *duetto*,) two; as two voices or instruments.

E, and; as *Moderato è Maestoso*, moderate and majestic.

Expressione, an expressive manner.

Expressivo, with expression.

Forte, (or *For.* or *F.*) loud.

Fortissimo, (or *F. F.*) very loud.

Forzando, (or *fz.*) implies that the notes over which it is placed is to be struck with particular force and held on.

Fugue, a piece in which one or more parts lead, and the rest follow in regular intervals.

Giusto, in an equal, steady and just time.

Grave, (or *Gravemente*,) denoting a time slower than *Largo*, but not so slow as *Adagio*.

Grazioso, a smooth, flowing and graceful style.

Largo, somewhat quicker than *Grave*.

Larghetto, not so slow as *Largo*.

Lamentevole, denotes that the movement over which it is placed is to be sung in a melancholy style.

Legato, signifies that the notes of the passage are to be performed in a close, smooth and gliding manner.

Lento, very slow.

Maestoso, with majesty.

Moderato, moderately.

Mezzo, half, middle, mean.

Mezzo Forte, moderately loud.

Mezzo Piano, rather soft.

Perdendosi, signifies a gradual decreasing of time to the last note; and a diminishing of tone, till entirely lost.

Piano, (or *Pia.*) soft.

Pianissimo, (or *P. P.*) very soft.

Poco, little; as *Poco piu lento*, a little slower; *Poco piu allegro*, a little quicker.

Quartetto, four voices, or instruments.

Quintetto, five voices, or instruments.

Sempre, always, throughout; as *sempre piano*, soft throughout.

Sicillano, a composition of $\frac{6}{4}$ or $\frac{6}{8}$, to be performed slowly and gracefully.

Solo, for a single voice or instrument.

Soprano, the Treble or higher voice part.

Sostenuto, a word implying that the notes are to be sustained, or held on to the extremity of their lengths.

Spirituoso, (or *Con Spirito*,) with spirit.

Staccato, notes to be staccated, must not be slurred, but performed in a distinct manner.

Symphony, a passage for instruments.

Tasto, no chords.

Tempo, time.

Trio, three voices or instruments.

Tutti, all; a word used in contradistinction to *Solo*.

Verse, one voice to a part.

Vivace, in a brisk and animated style.

INTRODUCTION TO THE ART OF SINGING,

OF THE STAFF.

MUSIC is written upon five parallel lines, with their intermediate spaces. These lines and spaces are called a Staff, and are counted upwards, from the lowest.

Example.

Lines. ⎰⁵⁴³²¹⎱   Spaces. ⎰⁴³²¹⎱

Every line or space, is called a degree: thus the Staff includes nine degrees, viz. five lines and four spaces. When more than nine degrees are wanted, the spaces below and above are used; and if a still greater compass is required, ledger lines are added either below or above the Staff.

Example.

Ledger lines above.

Ledger lines below.

2

There are seven original sounds in Music, and these are named from the first seven letters of the alphabet: viz. A, B, C, D, E, F, G. The application of these letters to the Staff is determined by a character called a Clef.

OF CLEFS.

There are three Clefs: viz. the Base, or F Clef; the Tenor, or C Clef; and the Treble, or G Clef. The Base Clef always denotes F, is placed upon the fourth line of the Staff, and is used for the lowest voices of men.

Example.   𝄢 F

The Tenor Clef always denotes C, and is placed either on the third or fourth line of the Staff.* When placed upon the third line, it is called the Alto, or Counter Tenor Clef, and is used for the highest voices of men.

* This Clef has formerly been used upon the first, second, and fifth, as well as upon the third and fourth line of the Staff.

Example.

When placed upon the fourth line, it is called the Tenor Clef, and is used for the middle voices of men.

Example.

The Treble Clef always denotes G, is placed upon the second line of the Staff, and is used for female voices.

Example.

The following example exhibits at one view the different Clefs with their relative situation ;

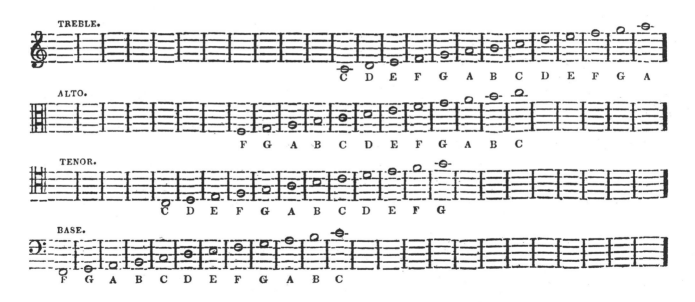

In many late publications, the C Clef has been omitted, and the F and G Clefs only have been used ; the latter being appropriated (though improperly) to the Tenor and Alto as well as to the Treble. This use of the G Clef has been necessarily adopted in the present work. The student will observe, however, that when the G Clef is used for Tenor or Alto, it denotes G an octave, or eight notes lower than when used in its proper place ; viz, for the Treble.*

The following example will exhibit at one view the Clefs used in this work, with their relative situation.

* This will explain some apparently forbidden progressions, as those intervals which appear to be a fifth above, are often in reality a fourth below.

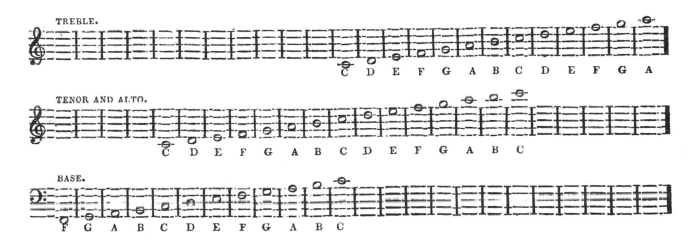

As it is of the greatest importance, that the situation of the letters upon the Staff, should be perfectly known, the student is advised to commit to memory, with great care, the following

GAMUT.

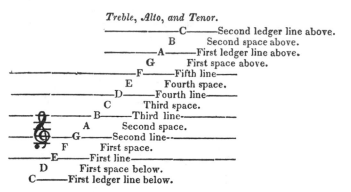

Treble, Alto, and Tenor.

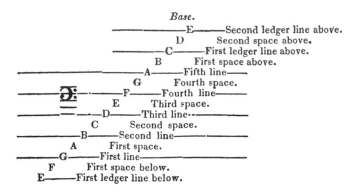

Base.

OF NOTES AND RESTS.

Notes are the representatives of sound: Rests are marks of silence; of these there are six kinds of each in modern use, as follows:

The Semibreve is a round white note: its rest is an oblong square, placed under a line.

The Minim is a white note with a stem: its rest is a square, placed above a line.

The Crotchet is a black note with a stem: its rest is a stem and hook turned to the right.

The Quaver is a black note with a stem and hook: its rest is a stem and hook turned to the left.

The Semiquaver is a black note with a stem and two hooks: its rest is a stem and two hooks turned to the left.

The Demisemiquaver is a black note with a stem and three hooks: its rest is a stem with three hooks turned to the left.

The proportion which the different notes bear to each other is exhibited in the following table :

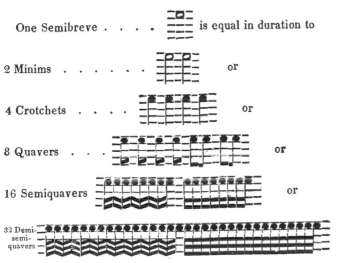

One Semibreve . . . . is equal in duration to

2 Minims . . . . . or

4 Crotchets . . . . or

8 Quavers . . . or

16 Semiquavers or

32 Demi-semi-quavers

Consequently one Minim is equal in duration to two Crotchets, one Crotchet to two Quavers, one Quaver to two Semiquavers, &c.

The Rests are equal in duration to their corresponding notes ; thus a Semibreve rest is equal to a Semibreve, a Minim rest is equal to a Minim, &c.

A Semibreve rest is used to fill a measure in all kinds of time.

A Dot after a note or rest adds one half to its original length : thus a dotted Semibreve is equal in duration to three Minims, a dotted Minim to three Crotchets, &c.

Example.

The figure 3 placed over or under three notes of the same kind, signifies that they are to be performed in the time of two notes of the same kind without the figure ; thus, three Crotchets with the figure 3 over them, are to be performed in the time of two Crotchets without the figure, &c.

Example.

The figure 6 placed over or under any six notes of the same kind, signifies that they are to be performed in the time of four notes of the same kind without the figure.

OF VARIOUS OTHER CHARACTERS USED IN MUSIC.

A Flat ♭ lowers a note half a tone.

A Sharp ♯ raises a note half a tone.

A Natural ♮ restores a note made flat or sharp to its original sound.

A Bar is used to divide the notes into equal measures.

A Double Bar or denote the end of a strain or movement, or of a line of the poetry.

A Brace shows how many parts belong to a score, or are to be performed together.

A Slur, or Tie, ⌣ is drawn over or under so many notes as are to be sung to one syllable.

A Repeat :S: or shows what part of a tune is to be sung twice.

The Double Ending **1 2** signifies that before repeating, the note under figure 1 is to be sung, and at repeating the note under figure 2, omitting the first, but when united by a tie, both are to be sung at repeating.

The Crescendo ◁ signifies a gradual increase of sound.

The Diminuendo ▷ signifies a gradual decrease of sound.

The Swell ◁▷ signifies a gradual increase and decrease of sound.

A Direct 𝄇 is employed at the end of a staff to show upon what degree the first note of the following staff is placed.

Staccato Marks ′′′′ ···· are placed over such notes as are to be performed in a very short and distinct manner.

Example.

The Shake *tr* is of all graces the most brilliant and elegant. It consists of a quick alternate repetition of the note above with that over which the character is placed, and usually ends with a turn from the note below.

Example.

The Appogiatura is a small note placed before a large one, from which it borrows its time. It is of the same value in duration of time with a large note of the same kind, and bears the same proportion to large notes as they do to each other, excepting when placed before a dotted note; then it takes the whole value of the note itself, and the note takes the time of the dot only. It always occurs on an accented part of a measure.

Example.

The After Note is a small note following a large one, from which it borrows its time. It always occurs on an unaccented part of a measure.

Example.

The Pause ⌢ leaves the time of a note or rest to be sustained at the pleasure of the performer.*

* It will add much to the effect of the Pause if a gradual swell and diminish is observed upon the note over which it is placed.

Syncopated, or Driving Notes, are those which commence on an unaccented, and are continued on an accented part of a measure.

Example.

OF SOLMIZATION, OR THE APPLICATION OF SYLLABLES TO THE NOTES.

In applying syllables to the different sounds, several different methods have been adopted.

The French use	ut, re, mi, fa, sol, la, si.
The Italians use	do, re, mi, fa, sol, la, si.
The English use	fa, sol, la, fa, sol, la, mi.

This last is the method usually adopted in this country.

The mi, upon which (according to this system) the other syllables depend, is itself dependent on the pitch of the octave, or key note, and changes with every modulation or change of key.

To find the mi, observe the following rule—

The natural place for mi is on B—

If B be flat mi is on	E	If F be sharp mi is on	F#
If B and E be flat mi is on	A	If F and C be sharp mi is on	C#
If B, E and A be flat mi is on	D	If F, C & G be sharp mi is on	G#
If B, E, A & D be flat mi is on	G	If F, C, G & D be sharp mi is on	D#

Having found the mi, above it are fa, sol, la, fa, sol, la—below it are la, sol, fa, la, sol, fa, and then mi occurs again either way.

From mi to fa and from la to fa are semitones, the rest are whole tones.

OF TIME.

By time in music is meant the duration and regularity of sound.

There are two kinds of time: viz. Common or equal, and Triple or unequal.

Simple Common Time has three signs :—

The first, 𝄴 contains one semibreve, or its equal in other notes or rests in a measure.—It has four beats, or motions, and is accented on the first and third parts of a measure.

Example.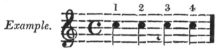

The second, 𝄵 contains one semibreve, or its equal in other notes or rests in a measure.—It has two beats, or motions, and is generally accented on the first part of a measure.

Example.

The third, 2/4 (which is also called half time) contains one minim, or its equal in other notes or rests in a measure.—It is beat and accented as the former.

Example.

Simple Triple Time has three signs :—

The first, 3/2 contains three minims, or their equal in other notes or rests in a measure.—It has three beats, or motions, and is accented principally on the first, and slightly on the third parts of a measure.

Example.

The second, 3/4 contains three crotchets, or their equal in other notes or rests in a measure.—It is beat and accented as the former.

Example.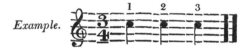

The third, 3/8 contains three quavers, or their equal in other notes or rests in a measure.—It is beat and accented as the former.

Example.

Compound Common Time has two signs :—

The first, 6/4 contains six crotchets, or their equal in other notes or rests in a measure. It has two beats, or motions, and is accented on the first and fourth parts of a measure.

Example.

The second, $\frac{6}{8}$ contains six quavers, or their equal in other notes or rests in a measure. It is beat and accented as the former.

Example.

Compound Triple Time has three signs: viz. $\frac{9}{4}$, $\frac{9}{8}$ and $\frac{9}{16}$.

They are found in the works of CORRELLI, HANDEL and others; but seldom occur in modern music.

The Semibreve (being now the longest note in common use) is made the general standard of reckoning, therefore when figures are employed as signs of time, those figures express the fractional parts of a semibreve contained in each measure; as $\frac{3}{4}$, three crotchets; $\frac{3}{8}$, three quavers, &c.

On the subject of beating time Dr. ARNOLD makes the following remark :—" I am by no means an advocate for the smallest motion or gesticulation, either with the hand, foot, or head, when a per-former once begins to play with any degree of exactness ; but, at the commencement, it is absolutely necessary that the right hand should be taught to make the beats in every measure, till it becomes to the pupil what the pendulum is to the clock, which is to keep it regular and in exact motion."

The natural scale of music is called Diatonic, and is a gradual succession of eight regular sounds, including five whole tones and two semitones. The whole doctrine of melody or tune, depends on rightly understanding the application of the two semitones and their places in the scale. These vary according to the mode.

There are two modes, Major and Minor. In the Major; the semitones are always found (ascending from the Tonic or Key note) between the third and fourth, and between the seventh and eighth intervals. The only natural series of this mode is that which commences with C.

Example of the Diatonic Scale in the Major Mode of C.

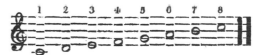

In the Minor, the semitones are found between the second and third, and between the fifth and sixth intervals. The only natural series of this mode is that which commences with A.

3

Example of the Diatonic Scale in the Minor Mode of A.

In the Minor Mode, the ascending scale and the descending scale, differ.

In the ascending scale, the seventh is raised a semitone as the proper Leading Note to the Octave. This leaves the interval, between the sixth and seventh, a tone and a half; but as the Diatonic scale must consist of tones and semitones, the sixth is also sharped, and the harsh interval of the extreme sharp second, avoided. Thus the ascending scale of the minor mode is artificial, and is formed with two notes altered from the Signature.

But in the descending scale the Seventh or Leading Note, is depressed a semitone to accommodate the sixth, and the natural scale of the signature remains unaltered.

Examples of the Ascending and Descending Scale in the Minor Mode.

The seven notes (for the eighth is but a repetition of the first) which form the Diatonic Scale of any Key in either Mode, have each a peculiar character and situation.

The first or Key Note is called the Tonic, because it regulates the time of the Octave, and upon it all the other notes depend.

The second (always counting upwards from the tonic) is called the Supertonic, from its being the next above.

The third is called the Mediante; from its being the middle way between the Tonic and the Dominante. It varies according to the mode, being the great third in the Major, and the little third in the Minor. It is much the most important interval in the Diatonic Scalé, since upon it depends the nature of the Mode; the Major being always accompanied with the great third, consisting of five semitones; and the Minor being always accompanied with the little third, consisting of four semitones.

The fourth is called the Subdominante, from its being a fifth below the Tonic.

The fifth is called the Dominante, from its importance in the Scale, and its immediate connexion with the Tonic.

The sixth is called the Submediante, from its being the middle way between the Tonic and Subdominante descending. Like the Mediante it varies with the Mode, being the great sixth in the Major, and the little sixth in the Minor.

The seventh is called the Sensible, or Leading Note, because upon hearing it the ear naturally anticipates the Tonic.

The last note in the Base is always the Tonic—if it be the first above the *Mi*, it is the Major Mode ; if it be the first below the *Mi*, it is the Minor Mode. The Major Tonic is always the note above the last sharp, or the fourth note below the last flat.— The Minor Tonic is always the note below the last sharp, or the third note above the last flat.

In consequence of the unequal division of the Diatonic Scale (consisting of tones and semitones) fourteen intervals are formed : —viz.—Unison, Little Second, Great Second, Little Third, Great Third, Perfect Fourth, Sharp Fourth, or Tritone, Flat Fifth, Perfect Fifth, Little Sixth, Great Sixth, Little Seventh, Great Seventh, and Octave.

Example of the Fourteen Diatonic Intervals.

Unison. Little 2d. Great 2d. Little 3d. Great 3d. Perfect 4th. Sharp 4th. Flat 5th. Perfect 5th. Little 6th. Great 6th. Little 7th. Great 7th. Octave.

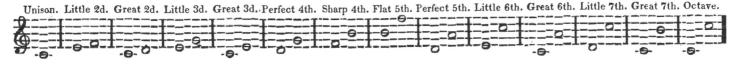

When the lowest note of an interval is placed an octave higher, or when the highest note of an interval is placed an octave lower, such change is called Inversion. Thus by inversion a

Second   becomes a Seventh   a

Third   becomes a Sixth   a

Fourth   becomes a Fifth   a

Fifth   becomes a Fourth   a

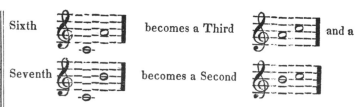

Sixth   becomes a Third   and a

Seventh   becomes a Second

The Diatonic Intervals are also consonant or dissonant. The octave, fifth, fourth, thirds, and sixths, being agreeable to the ear, are called consonant; and the seconds, sevenths, and sharp fourth, being less pleasing, are called dissonant.

By a division of the Diatonic scale, ascending by sharps, and descending by flats, a scale is formed of semitones only, which is called Chromatic.

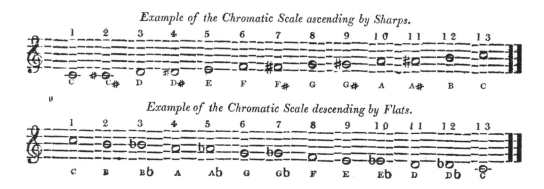

Example of the Chromatic Scale ascending by Sharps.

1 2 3 4 5 6 7 8 9 10 11 12 13

C C♯ D D♯ E F F♯ G G♯ A A♯ B C

Example of the Chromatic Scale descending by Flats.

1 2 3 4 5 6 7 8 9 10 11 12 13

C B B♭ A A♭ G G♭ F E E♭ D D♭ C

In this scale we have twelve distinct sounds, from each of which as a tonic, we may form the natural diatonic scale in either mode.

Here the utility of flats and sharps will appear evident to the student. Let him, for instance, take G as a tonic, and from it form the Diatonic scale in the major mode. He will find that in order to bring the semitone between the seventh and eighth notes, the seventh or F will require to be raised by a sharp one semitone.

Example of the Diatonic Scale in the Key of G major.

Or let him take F as a tonic, and from it form the Diatonic Scale in the major mode; he will find a flat required before the fourth, or B, that the semitone may be between the third and fourth.

Example of the Diatonic Scale in the Key of F.

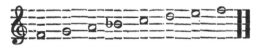

Or let him take E as a tonic, and from it form the Diatonic Scale in the minor mode; he will find a sharp before the second or F, necessary, that the semitone may be between the second and third.

Example of the Diatonic Scale in the Key of E minor.

Or let him take D as a tonic, and from it form the Diatonic Scale in the minor mode; he will find a flat required before B, that the semitone may be between the fifth and sixth.

Example of the Diatonic Scale in the Key of D minor.

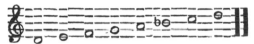

Every major key has its relative minor, and every minor key has its relative major.

The relative minor to any major key is its sixth above, or its third below; and the relative major to any minor key is its third above or its sixth below.

When, in the course of a melody or tune, the tonic is changed by the introduction of a flat or sharp, such change is called Modulation.

The most natural and easy modulations are the following, viz. 1st. From any tonic to its dominant. This is done by the introduction of a new sharp upon the subdominant of the key, which becomes a leading note; the supertonic becomes the dominant, and the tonic itself becomes the dominant seventh, to the new key.

Example of a modulation from the key of C to its dominant.

2d. From any tonic to its subdominant. This is done by the introduction of a new flat upon the leading note of the key, which becomes a dominant seventh; the tonic itself becomes the dominant, and the mediant becomes the leading note, to the new key.

Example of a modulation from the key of C to its subdominant.

These changes are in constant use, and occur in almost every psalm tune.

The observations that have been made upon the Diatonic and Chromatic scales, the major and minor mode, modulation, &c. perhaps rather more properly belong to musical science than to the mere art of learning to sing. To such as wish to become acquainted with the theory of music, Callcott's Musical Grammar, and Kollman's Essay on Musical Harmony, are recommended as the best works that have been published in this country.

LESSONS FOR THE EXERCISE OF THE VOICE.

G Major ascending and descending.

G Minor ascending and descending.

fa, sol, la, fa,   sol, la, mi, fa,   fa, mi, la, sol,   fa, la, sol, fa.   la, mi, fa, sol,   la, fa, sol, la,   la, sol, fa, la,   sol, fa, mi, la.

Page   *ERRATA.*

32. The last note on F, third measure in the Air, should be on G.

71. First staff of the Air, first measure, the last note on C, should be on A.

83. Second Alto staff, second measure, the last note on D, should be on C.

99. The sign of the time should be $\frac{3}{2}$.

117. First Tenor staff, third measure, the last quaver but one on B, should be on C.

176. Lower Base staff, fifth measure, the minim on C, should be on E.

217. First Brace, the movement should have been signed $\frac{2}{4}$.

260. Lower Treble staff, fifth measure, the crotchet on C, should be on D.

THE

BOSTON HANDEL AND HAYDN SOCIETY

COLLECTION OF CHURCH MUSIC.

OLD HUNDRED. L. M. Martin Luther.

Be thou, O God, exalted high, And as thy glory fills the sky, So let it be on earth display'd, Till thou art here as there obey'd.

4

OWENS. L. M. 6 lines.

Mozart.

Sostenuto Adagio.

Lord, when my thoughts de - light - ed rove, Amidst the won-ders of thy love, Sweet hope re - vives my droop-ing heart, And

bids my fears and doubts de - part. Lord, so my thoughts de - light - ed rove, Amidst the won-ders of thy love.

MORNING HYMN. L. M. 6 lines. Costellow.

Soon as the morn sa-lutes your eyes, And, from sweet sleep, re-fresh'd you rise, Think on the Au-thor of the light,

And praise him for the glo-rious sight! His mer-cy in-fi-nite a-dore, His good-ness in-fi-nite im-plore.

ANGELS' HYMN. L. M.

Tansur.

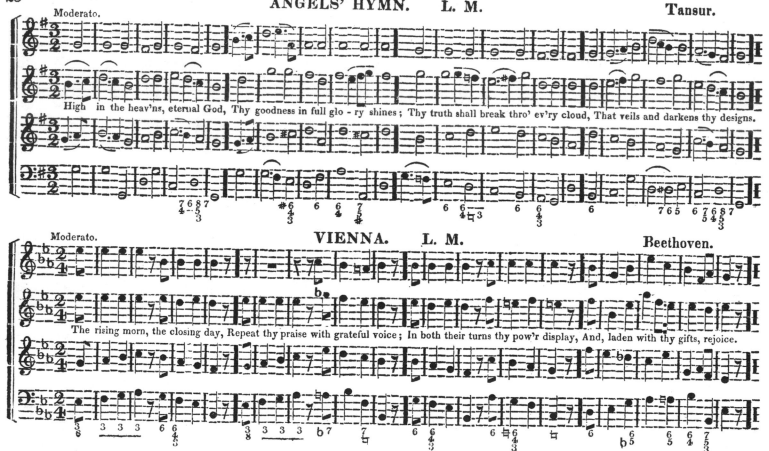

Moderato.

High in the heav'ns, eternal God, Thy goodness in full glo - ry shines; Thy truth shall break thro' ev'ry cloud, That veils and darkens thy designs.

VIENNA. L. M.

Beethoven.

Moderato.

The rising morn, the closing day, Repeat thy praise with grateful voice; In both their turns thy pow'r display, And, laden with thy gifts, rejoice.

O could I soar to worlds a - bove, The blest a - bode of peace and love,

How glad - ly would I mount and fly, On an - gels' wings, To worlds on high!

St. PETER's. L. M.

Harwood.

To God the great, the ev - er blest, Let songs of hon - our be ad - - drest;

His mer - cy firm for - ev - er stands, Give him the thanks his love de - mands.

Legato.

Up to the fields where an-gels lie, And liv-ing wa-ters gent-ly roll; Fain would my thoughts as-cend on high, But sin hangs heavy on my soul.

WINCHESTER.　L. M.　　　　　　　　Dr. Croft.

Maestoso.

My God, ac-cept my ear-ly vows, Like morn-ing in-cense, in thy house; And let my night-ly wor-ship rise, Sweet as the ev'-ning sac-ri-fice.

ISLINGTON. L. M.

This life's a dream, an emp-ty show, But the bright world to which I go,

Hath joys sub-stan-tial and sin-cere, When shall I wake, When shall I wake, and find me there.

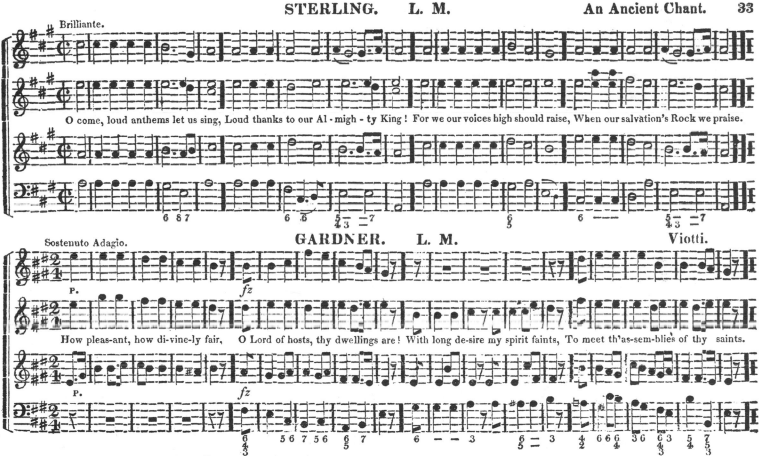

O come, loud anthems let us sing, Loud thanks to our Al-migh-ty King! For we our voices high should raise, When our salvation's Rock we praise.

GARDNER. L. M. Viotti.

How pleas-ant, how di-vine-ly fair, O Lord of hosts, thy dwellings are! With long de-sire my spirit faints, To meet th'as-sem-blies of thy saints.

5

BATH. L. M.

Moderato.

Life is the time to serve the Lord, The time t'insure the great reward; And while the lamp holds out to burn, The vilest sin - ner may return.

6 6 8 7   #6   6   6   6   6   6 5   6   7
   5   4   4   4   4   3
               3   3

SEASONS. L. M.

Pleyel.

Dolce.

Thy goodness, Lord, doth crown the year, Thy paths drop fatness all around; And barren wilds thy praise declare, And vo-cal hills re-turn the sound.

7 5 6 6 7 7   7 5 6 5   8 7   8 7   6 7 5 6 6 7 7
        5   5

Moderato.

My soul, in- spir'd with sac - red love, God's ho - ly name for - ev - er bless;

Of all his fa - vours mind - ful prove, And still thy grate - ful thanks ex - press.

POLAND. L. M. 6 lines.

Wranizky.

Maestoso.

O God, my strength, my soul's de - sire, To thee my heart and voice as - pire; For thou art good, as well as great,

And mer - cy is thy judg-ment seat. O God, my King, with ho - ly fire, My heart and voice to thee as - pire.

GLOUCESTER. L. M. 6 lines. Milgrove. 87

Angels of light, e - the - real fires! A - rise and sweep your aw-ful lyres! To you the sac - red right be - longs,

To raise the lay, and lead our songs. Ye in his courts of glo - ry dwell, And best his pow'r and grace can tell.

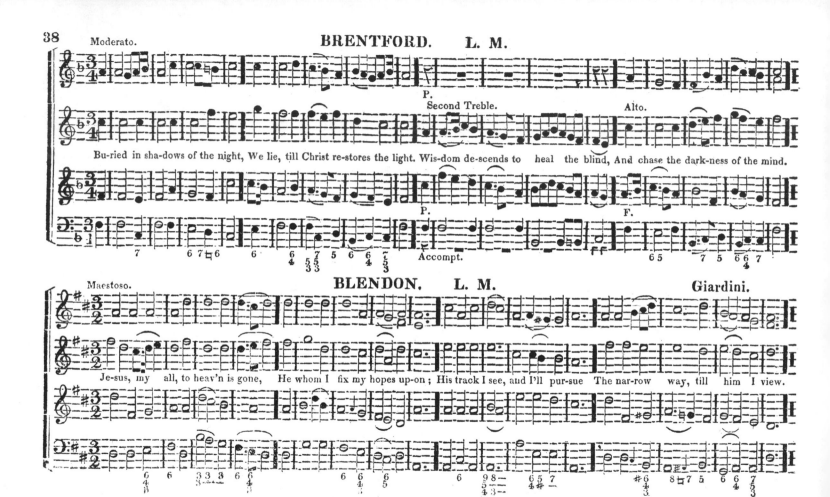

BRENTFORD. L. M.

Bu-ried in sha-dows of the night, We lie, till Christ re-stores the light. Wis-dom de-scends to heal the blind, And chase the dark-ness of the mind.

BLENDON. L. M.

Je-sus, my all, to heav'n is gone, He whom I fix my hopes up-on; His track I see, and I'll pur-sue The nar-row way, till him I view.

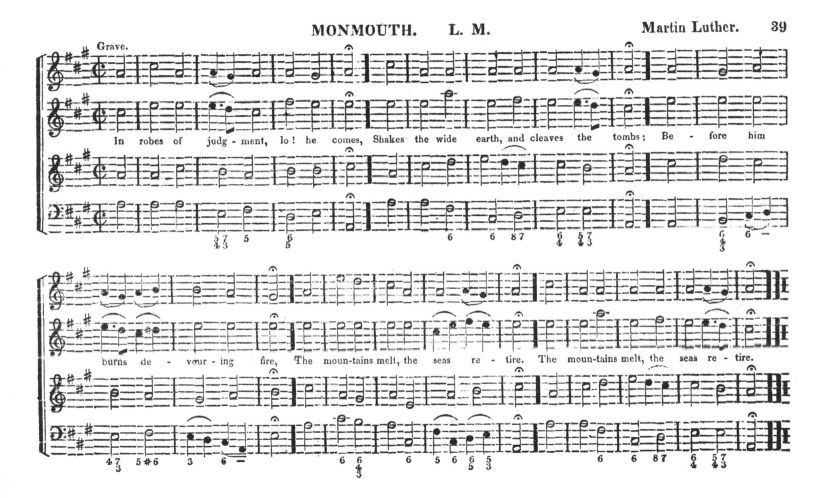

In robes of judg-ment, lo! he comes, Shakes the wide earth, and cleaves the tombs; Be - fore him

burns de - vour-ing fire, The moun-tains melt, the seas re - tire. The moun-tains melt, the seas re - tire.

PORTSMOUTH. L. M.

Gelineck.

Andante.

Indulgent still to my request, How free thy tender mercies are! With full consent my thoughts attest, My gracious God, thy faithful care.

ROTHWELL. L. M.

Moderato.

Praise ye the Lord, let praise employ, In his own courts, your songs of joy! The spacious firmament around, Shall echo back, Shall echo back the joyful sound.

WINCHELSEA. L. M. — Prelleur.

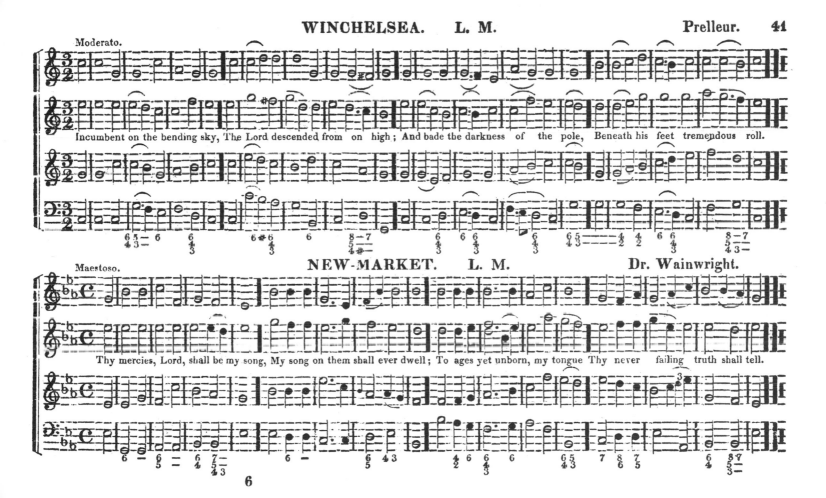

Incumbent on the bending sky, The Lord descended from on high; And bade the darkness of the pole, Beneath his feet tremendous roll.

Thy mercies, Lord, shall be my song, My song on them shall ever dwell; To ages yet unborn, my tongue Thy never failing truth shall tell.

NEW-MARKET. L. M. — Dr. Wainwright.

6

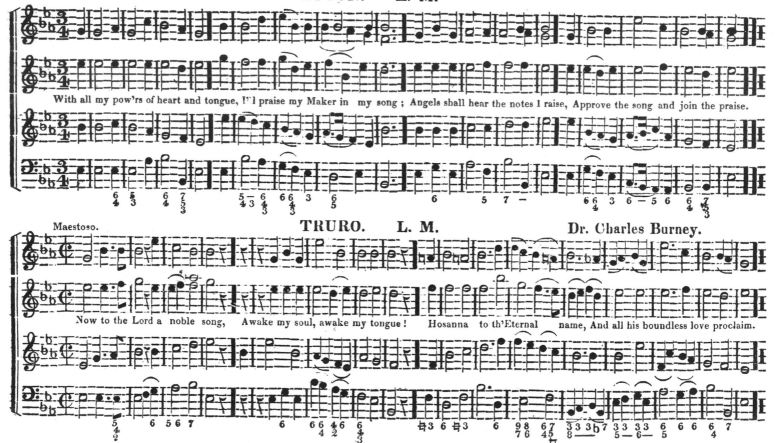

42

LUTON. L. M.

With all my pow'rs of heart and tongue, I'l praise my Maker in my song ; Angels shall hear the notes I raise, Approve the song and join the praise.

TRURO. L. M.   Dr. Charles Burney.

Maestoso.

Now to the Lord a noble song,   Awake my soul, awake my tongue !   Hosanna to th'Eternal   name, And all his boundless love proclaim.

There is a stream, whose gentle course Surrounds the cit - y of our God. There is a stream, whose gentle course

Surrounds the cit - y of our God—A sac - red riv - er, from whose fount, The liv - ing wa - ters flow abroad.

EVENING HYMN. L. M.

Tallis.

Moderato.

Glo-ry to thee, my God, this night, For all the blessings of the light; Keep me, O keep me, King of kings, Beneath thine own Almighty wings!

GERMANY. L. M.

Beethoven

Adagio é sempre piano.

Softly the shade of ev'ning falls, Sprinkling the earth with dewy tears; While nature's voice to slumber calls, And silence reigns amid the spheres.

Allegretto.

fz

Lord, in thy great, thy glorious name, I place my hope, my on - ly trust: Save me from sorrow,

Tasto.

fz

guilt and shame, Thou ev - er gra - cious, ev - er just. Thou ev - er gracious, ev - er just.

Second Treble.

Alto.

Tasto.

NEW SABBATH.   L. M.

Isaac Smith.

For thee, O God, our con-stant praise, In Zi - on waits, thy cho - sen seat;

Our prom - is'd al - tars we will raise, And there our zeal - ous vows com - plete.

ELLENTHORPE. L. M. Linley.

Lyrics (MEDWAY): My God, permit me not to be, A stranger to myself and thee! Amidst ten thousand tho'ts I rove, Forgetful of my highest love.

Lyrics (ELLENTHORPE, verse 1): Say, how may earth and heav'n unite? And how shall man with angels join? What link harmonious may be found, Discordant natures to combine.

Lyrics (ELLENTHORPE, verse 2): Loud swell the pealing organs notes! Breathe forth your souls in raptures high! In praises men with angels join;—Music's the language of the sky.

WESTON. L. M.

Beethoven.

Now night in silent grandeur reigns, And holds the slumb'ring world in chains; Pale from the cloud the

moon-beam steals, And half cre - a - tion's face re - veals. And half cre - a - tion's face re - veals.

How sweet thy dwellings, Lord, how fair, What peace, what bliss, inhabit there. With ardent hope, with strong desire,

My heart, my flesh to thee aspire; I burn to tread thy courts, and thee, My God, the living God, to see.

CAMDEN. L. M. 2 verses.

Mozart.

Andantino.

The saffron tints of morn appear, And glow across the blushing east; The brilliant orb of day is near,

To dis-si-pate the ling'ring mist; And while his mantling splendors dart, Their radiance o'er the kindling skies,

To chase the darkness of my heart, A - rise, O God of light, a - rise, a - rise, a - rise, a - rise.

ALL SAINTS.　L. M.

Moderato.

God of the Sabbath, hear our vows, On this thy day, within thy house! And own, as grateful sac - ri - fice, The songs which in thy tem-ple rise!

PARK STREET. L. M.

Venua.

Cantabile.

Hark! how the choral song of heav'n, Swells full of peace and joy, a - bove! Hark! how they strike their golden harps, And raise the tuneful notes of love! And raise the tuneful notes of love.

Cantabile é Sostenuto.

With ho-ly fear and hum-ble song, The dread-ful God, our souls a-dore; Rev'-rence and awe be-come the tongue That

speaks the ter-rors of his pow'r. Rev'-rence and awe be-come the tongue That speaks the ter-rors of his pow'r.

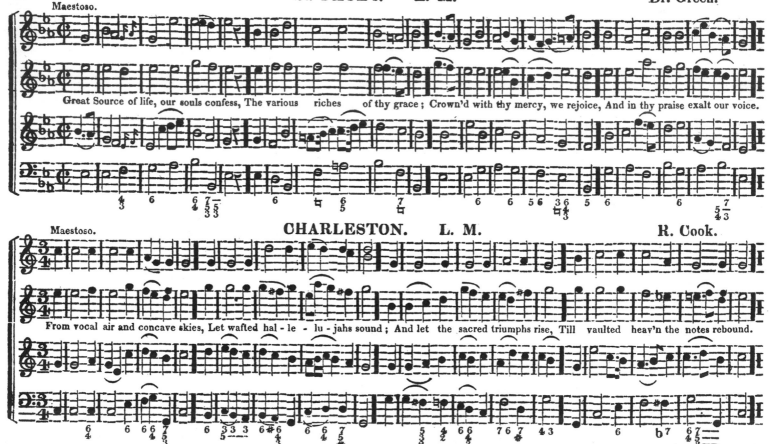

St. PAUL's. L. M.   Dr. Green.

Maestoso.

Great Source of life, our souls confess, The various riches of thy grace; Crown'd with thy mercy, we rejoice, And in thy praise exalt our voice.

CHARLESTON. L. M.   R. Cook.

Maestoso.

From vocal air and concave skies, Let wafted hal - le - lu - jahs sound; And let the sacred triumphs rise, Till vaulted heav'n the notes rebound.

Lord, thou hast known my inmost mind, Thou dost my path and bed inclose; My wak-ing soul on thee relies,

On thee my sleeping thoughts repose: Where from thy presence can I fly, - - - - - Lord, ever present ever nigh?

WESTVILLE. L. M. 6 lines.

Klose.

Moderato.

My God, in thee are all the springs, In which my comfort can arise; I seek the shadow of thy wings,

7 5   6 7   7 6   7   5 7   4 6 5 = 6 6 3 6
        4 5   2
          4 3   4

When gath'ring clouds obscure the skies. I seek the shadow of thy wings, When gath'ring clouds obscure the skies.

♮6 6 6 6   6   7   7 3 87 5 3   6 7=   4 6 6   6 6   6 7
        ♮   4 5   2 4   5   4 5
                                     4 3   3

Alto. Fuge. Allegro.

Treble. We bless the Lord, the Lord, the just, the good, Who fills our hearts with joy and food;

Base. We bless the Lord, we bless the Lord, the just, the good, Who fills our hearts with joy and food;

We bless the Lord, &c.

Who pours his blessings from the skies, And loads our days with rich sup - - plies.

Who pours his bles - - sings from the skies, And loads our days with rich sup - - plies.

Who pours, &c.

8

EATON. L. M. 6 lines.

Wyvill.

Allegretto.

A - wake our souls, a - way our fears, Let ev'ry trembling thought be gone ! A - wake, and run the heav'nly race,

Second Treble.

Alto.

And put a cheerful courage on ! A - wake, and run the heav'nly race, And put a cheerful courage on !

Softly the shade of ev'ning falls, Sprinkling the earth with dewy tears; While nature's

voice to slum - ber calls, And silence reigns a - mid the spheres—a - mid the spheres.

WATSON'S. L. M.

O Thou, to whose all - search - ing sight, The dark - ness shin - eth as the light;

Search, prove my heart, it pants for thee, O burst these bonds, and set me free.

Moderato.

At anchor laid, remote from home, Toiling I cry, sweet spirit come. Celestial breeze, no longer stay, But swell my sails, and speed my way.

Second Treble. P. Alto. F.

P. Tasto. F.

DUKE-STREET. L. M. J. Hatton.

Moderato.

Lord, when thou didst ascend on high, Ten thousand angels fill'd the sky; Those heav'nly guards around thee wait, Like chariots that attend thy state.

ALBANY. L. M.

Dr. Hayes.

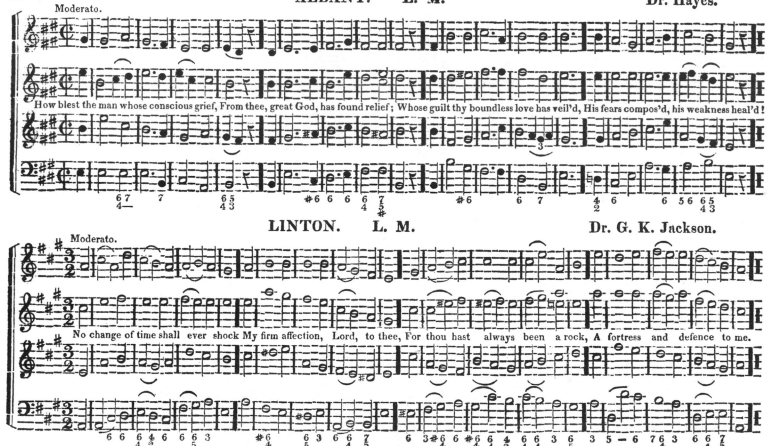

How blest the man whose conscious grief, From thee, great God, has found relief; Whose guilt thy boundless love has veil'd, His fears compos'd, his weakness heal'd!

LINTON. L. M.

Dr. G. K. Jackson.

No change of time shall ever shock My firm affection, Lord, to thee, For thou hast always been a rock, A fortress and defence to me.

Thou Lamb of God, thou Prince of Peace, For thee my thirs - ty soul doth pine; My long-ing

heart im - plores thy grace, Oh! make me in thy like-ness shine! Oh! make me in thy like - ness shine!

SURRY. L. M.

Costellow.

No more fa - tigue, no more dis - tress, Nor sin nor death shall reach the place; No groans shall mingle

with the songs, Which war - ble from im - mor - tal tongues. Which war - ble from im - mor - tal tongues.

Moderato.

The hope of sin - ners lies be - low, 'Tis all the hap - pi - ness they know;

'Tis all they seek; they take their shares, And leave the rest— And leave the rest a - mong their heirs.

9

RICHMOND. L. M. 2 verses.

De La Main.

When we, our wearied limbs to rest, Sat down by proud Eu - phra - tes' stream ; We wept, with doleful

thoughts op - prest, And Si - on was our mourn-ful theme. Our harps, that, when with joy we sung, Were wont their

tune-ful parts to bear, With si-lent strings ne-glect-ed hung, On wil-low trees that wither'd there.

NORFOLK. **L. M.** J. Ashton.

Moderato.

Amidst these various scenes of ills, Each stroke some kind design fulfils ; And shall I murmur at my lot, When sov'reign love directs the rod ?

ZION HILL. L. M. 2 verses.

The first six bars are by STERKEL ; the remainder by I. WHITAKER, author of The Seraph, &c.

Andante é mezzo forte.

Jesus, where'er thy people meet, There they behold thy mercy seat; Where'er they seek thee thou art found, And

ev'ry place is hallow'd ground; For thou, within no walls confin'd, In - hab - i - test the hum - ble mind; Such

ev - er bring thee where they come, And going take thee to their home. For thou, within no walls confin'd, In-

hab - i - test the humble mind ; Such ev - er bring thee where they come, And going take thee to their home.

HAMDEN. L. M. 6 lines.

Mozart.

Eternal Rul - er of the skies, How various are thy works, how wise! How great the wonders

thou hast wrought, And deep be - yond all search of thought!

Organ.

E-ter-nal Rul-er of the skies, How various are thy works, how wise!

St. GEORGE's. L. M.

Retire, O sleep, from ev'ry eye! The rising morning re-ap-pears; The sun ascends the dappled sky, And drinks cre-a-tion's dewy tears.

PROCTOR. L. M.

Thus saith the high and lof-ty One, I sit up-on my ho-ly throne, My name is God, I

dwell on high, Dwell in mine own e-ter-ni-ty. Dwell in mine own e-ter-ni-ty.

GEORGETOWN. L. M.

To thee, O God, with-out de-lay, Will I my morning hom-age pay; For thee I

long, for thee I look, So pil-grims seek the cool-ing brook. So pil-grims seek the cool-ing brook.

10

FRAMINGHAM. L. M. 6 lines.

Pleyel.

Father of mer - cies, God of love! Oh! hear a hum - ble suppliant's cry; Bend from thy

lof - ty seat a - bove, Thy throne of glorious maj - es - ty! Oh! deign to lis - ten

to my voice, And bid this drooping heart re - joice! And bid this droop-ing heart re - joice!

GREEN's HUNDREDTH. L. M. Dr. Green.

Moderato.

Sweet is the work, my God, my King, To praise thy name, give thanks and sing; To shew thy love by morning light, And talk of all thy truth at night.

AUGUSTA. L. M. 2 verses.

Gluck.

From all that dwell be - low the skies, Let the Cre - a - tor's praise a - rise: Let the Re-deem-er's name be sung,

From ev'ry land, by ev'ry tongue! E - ter - nal are thy mercies, Lord, E - ter - nal truth at - tends thy word;

Thy praise shall sound from shore to shore, Till suns shall set and rise no more. Till suns shall set and rise no more.

CHAPEL-STREET.   L. M.   Mather.

Moderato.

Second Treble. P.   Alto. F.

E - ter - nal Source of ev'ry joy, Well may thy praise our lips employ ; While in thy temple we appear, Thy goodness crowns the circling year.

P.   F.

PERGOLESI. L. M.

Pergolesi.

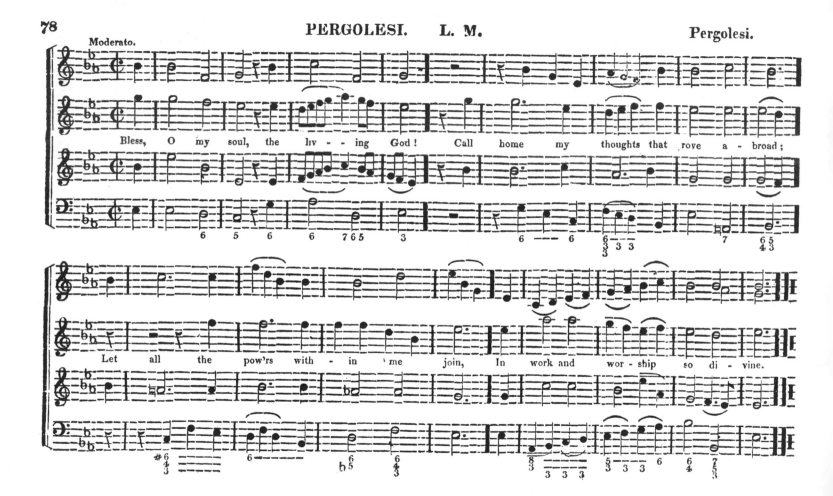

Bless, O my soul, the liv — — ing God! Call home my thoughts that rove a - broad;

Let all the pow'rs with - in 'me join, In work and wor - ship so di - vine.

The King of saints, how fair his face, A - dorn'd with maj - es - ty and grace!

He comes with bles - sings from a - bove, And wins the na - tions to his love.

ARMLEY. L. M.

Lamentevole.

Now let our mournful songs re - cord, The dy - ing sor - rows of our Lord;

When he com - plain'd in tears and blood, As one for - sak - en of his God.

Moderato.

When 'mid the gloom of night I stray, And heav'n's re - splend - ent arch sur - vey—And mark with rapture and sur-

prise, The va - ried glo - ries of the skies, Ah ! what is man ! thou great Su - preme, That thou should stoop to vis - it him ?

11

EVENING HYMN. L. M.

Jer. Clark.

Grave.

Sleep, downy sleep, come close my eyes, Tir'd with beholding vanities! Welcome, sweet sleep, that driv'st away, The toils and follies of the day!

AVERNO. L. M.

Dr. Hayes.

Grave.

My humbled soul its crimes shall own, Behold me bow before thy throne; To thee my inmost guilt disclose, And in thy bosom pour my woes.

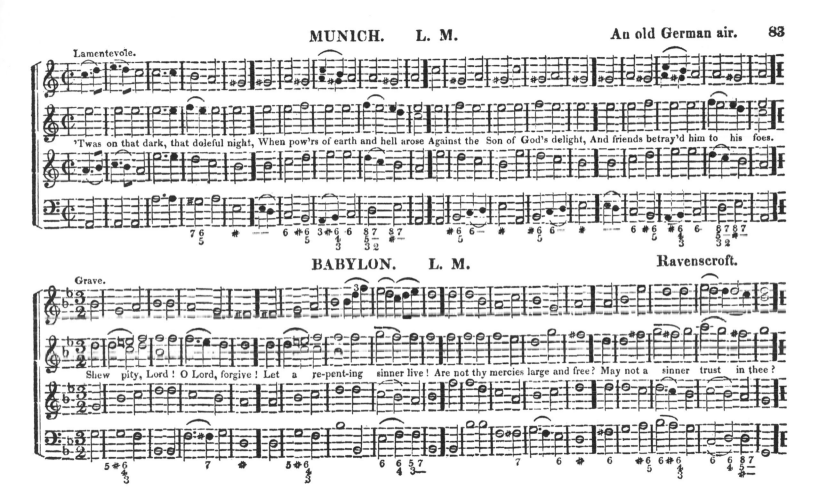

MUNICH.   L. M.

An old German air.   **83**

Lamentevole.

'Twas on that dark, that doleful night, When pow'rs of earth and hell arose Against the Son of God's delight, And friends betray'd him to his foes.

BABYLON.   L. M.

Ravenscroft.

Grave.

Shew pity, Lord! O Lord, forgive! Let a re-pent-ing sinner live! Are not thy mercies large and free? May not a sinner trust in thee?

DARWEN. L. M.

Affettuoso.

Who from the shades of gloomy night, When the last tear of hope is shed,

Can bid the soul re - turn to light, And break the slum - ber of the dead?

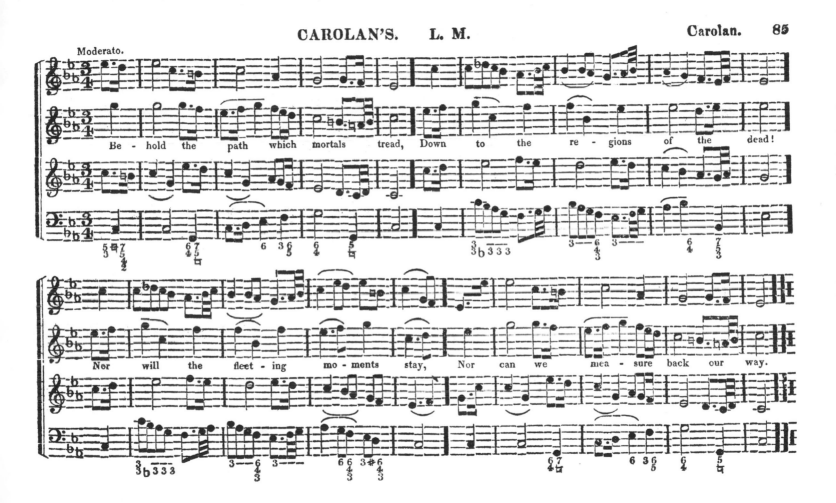

Be - hold the path which mortals tread, Down to the re - gions of the dead!

Nor will the fleet - ing mo - ments stay, Nor can we mea - sure back our way.

WESTBURY. L. M.

Grave.

Prelleur.

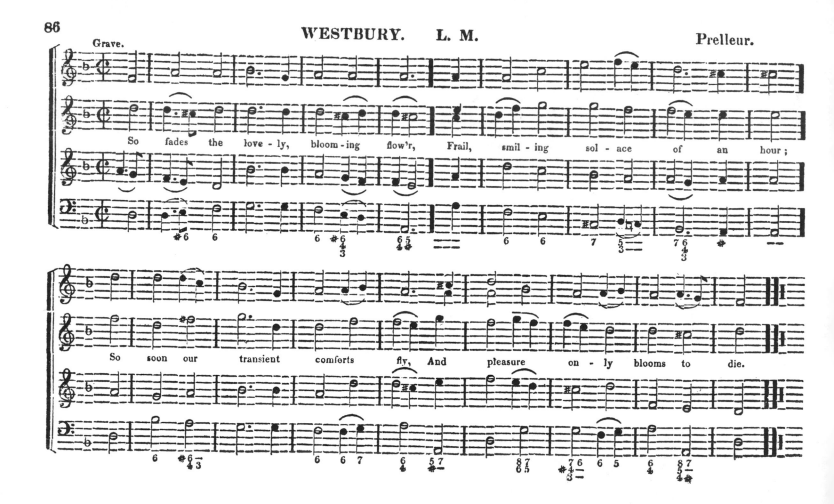

So fades the love - ly, bloom - ing flow'r, Frail, smil - ing sol - ace of an hour;

So soon our transient comforts fly, And pleasure on - ly blooms to die.

In mem'ry of your dy - ing Lord, Do this, he said, till time shall end,

Meet at my ta - ble and re - cord, The love of your de - part - ed Lord.

St. MATTHEW's.   C. M.   2 verses.   Dr. Croft.

"Let heav'n arise, let earth appear!" Said the Almighty Lord: The heav'ns arose, the earth appear'd, At his cre - a - ting word.

Thick darkness brooded o'er the deep: God said, "Let there be light!" The light shone round with smiling ray, And scatter'd ancient night.

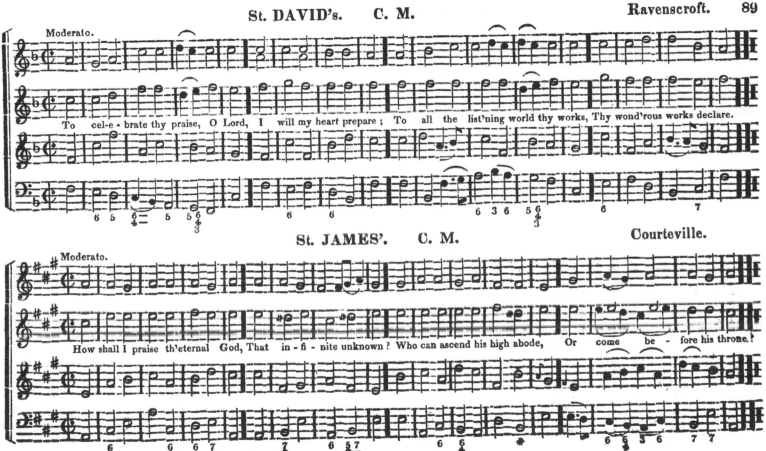

St. DAVID's.   C. M.   Ravenscroft.   89

Moderato.

To cel-e-brate thy praise, O Lord, I will my heart prepare; To all the list'ning world thy works, Thy wond'rous works declare.

St. JAMES'.   C. M.   Courteville.

Moderato.

How shall I praise th'eternal God, That in-fi-nite unknown? Who can ascend his high abode, Or come be-fore his throne.?

12

STEPHENS. C. M.

Jones.

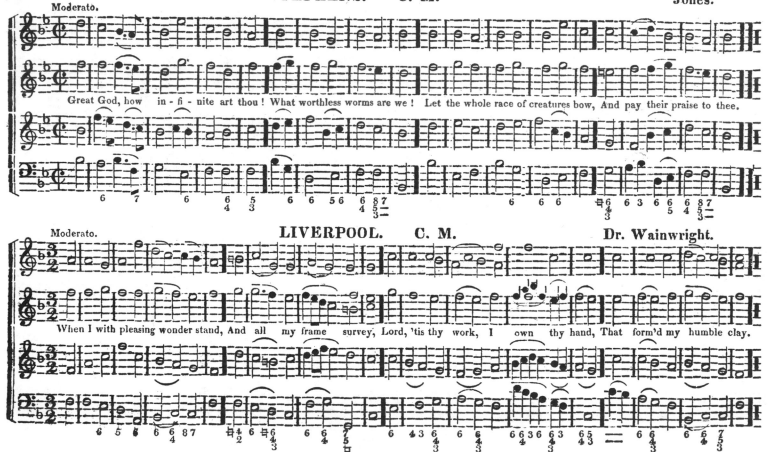

Great God, how in-fi-nite art thou! What worthless worms are we! Let the whole race of creatures bow, And pay their praise to thee.

LIVERPOOL. C. M.

Dr. Wainwright.

When I with pleasing wonder stand, And all my frame survey, Lord, 'tis thy work, I own thy hand, That form'd my humble clay.

Jesus, I love thy charming name, 'Tis music to my ear; Fain would I sound it out so loud, That earth and heav'n should hear.

CANTERBURY.   C. M.   Ravenscroft.

O thou, from whom all goodness flows, I lift my heart to thee; In all my sorrows, conflicts, woes, Dear Lord, remember me !

St. ANNS.   C. M.
Dr. Croft.

Moderato.

My God, my portion and my love, My ev - er - last - ing all! I've none but thee in heav'n above, Or on this earthly ball.

HOWARDS.   C. M.
Mrs. Cuthbert.

Moderato.

Lord, hear the voice of my complaint, Accept my secret pray'r; To thee, alone, my King, my God, Will I for help repair.

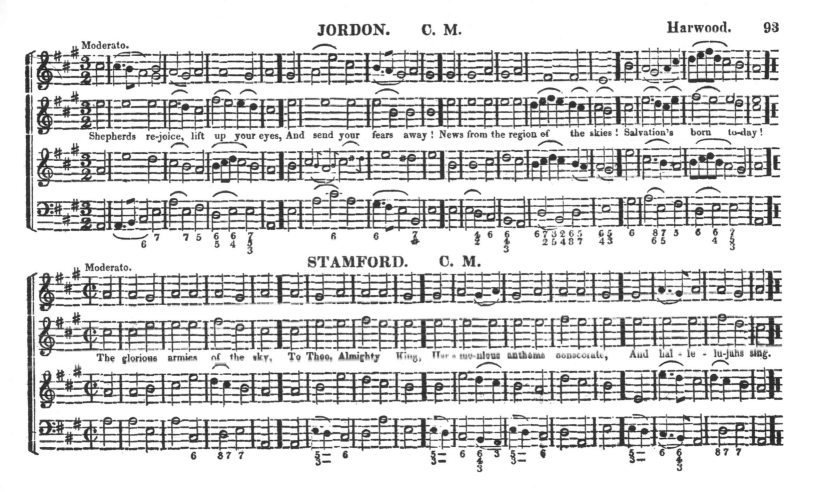

JORDON.   C. M.   Harwood.   93

Shepherds re-joice, lift up your eyes, And send your fears away! News from the region of the skies! Salvation's born to-day!

STAMFORD.   C. M.

The glorious armies of the sky, To Thee, Almighty King, Har-mo-nious anthems consecrate, And hal-le-lu-jahs sing.

Thou art my portion, O my God, Soon as I know thy way, My heart makes haste t'obey thy word, And suffers no de-lay.

I choose the path of heav'nly truth, And glory in my choice: Not all the riches of the earth, Could make me so rejoice.

CAMBRIDGE. C. M.
Dr. Randall.

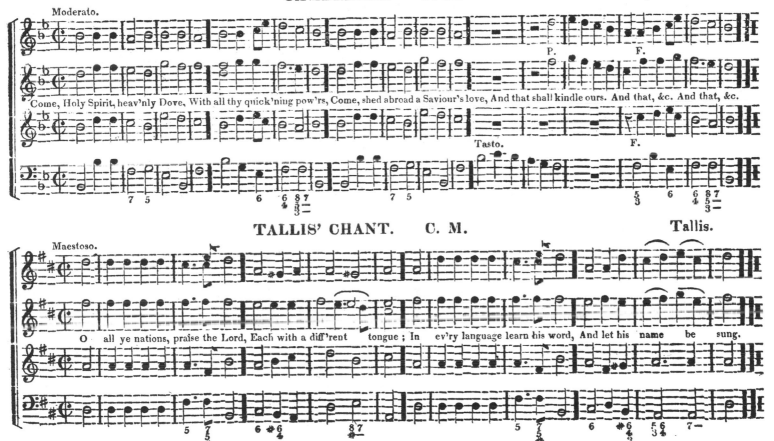

Come, Holy Spirit, heav'nly Dove, With all thy quick'ning pow'rs, Come, shed abroad a Saviour's love, And that shall kindle ours. And that, &c. And that, &c.

TALLIS' CHANT. C. M.
Tallis.

O all ye nations, praise the Lord, Each with a diff'rent tongue ; In ev'ry language learn his word, And let his name be sung.

NEW-YORK. C. M.

Dr. Blow.

Hap - - - py the man, whose grac - es reign, Where love in - spires the breast;

Love is the bright - est of the train, And per - fects all the rest.

NEWTON.   C. M.

Come, happy souls, approach your God With new melodious songs! Come, render to Al - migh - ty grace, The tribute of your tongues.

St. GREGORY's.   C. M.

Dr. Wainwright.

I'm not asham'd to own my Lord, Or   to defend his cause, Maintain the honour of his word, The glo - ry of his cross.

13

While thee I seek, pro-tect-ing Pow'r, Be my vain wishes still'd ; And may this con-se-crat-ed hour, With better hopes be fill'd !

Thy love the pow'r of thought bestow'd, To thee my thoughts would soar, Thy mercy o'er my life has flow'd, That mer - cy I adore.

As originally published by Dr. Arnold.

How large the promise, how divine, To Abr'ham and his seed! "I'll be a God to thee and thine, Sup-

ply - ing all their need." "I'll be a God to thee and thine, Sup - ply - ing all their need."

BLANDFORD. C. M.

T. Jackson.

Maestoso.

Awake, my soul, arise my tongue ! Prepare a tuneful voice, In God the life of all my joys, Aloud will I rejoice.

BRAY. C. M.

Moderato.

To God, our never-failing strength, With loud applauses sing ; And jointly make a cheerful noise, To Jacob's awful King ! To Jacob's awful King !

TEMPEST. C. M. 2 verses. Haydn. 101

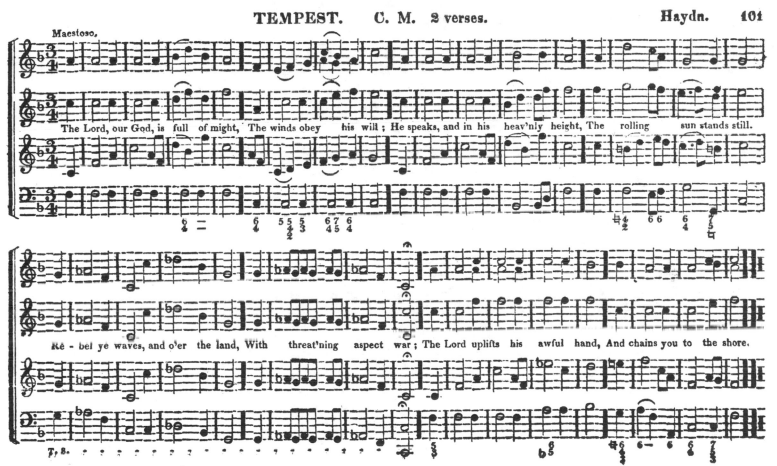

The Lord, our God, is full of might, The winds obey his will ; He speaks, and in his heav'nly height, The rolling sun stands still.

Re - bel ye waves, and o'er the land, With threat'ning aspect war ; The Lord uplifts his awful hand, And chains you to the shore.

St. JOHN's.   C. M.

Moderato.

Now to the Lamb that once was slain, Be end-less hon-ors paid ; Sal-va-tion, glo-ry, joy remains, For-ev-er on his head.

MESSIAH.   C. M.   Handel.

Sostenuto Adagio.

I know that my Re-deem-er lives, And ev-er prays for me ; Salvation to his saints he gives, And life and lib-er-ty.

Moderato.

O Thou, to whom all crea - tures bow, With - in this earth - ly frame,

'Thro' all the world how great art Thou, How glorious is thy name!

SWANWICK. C. M.

Lucas,

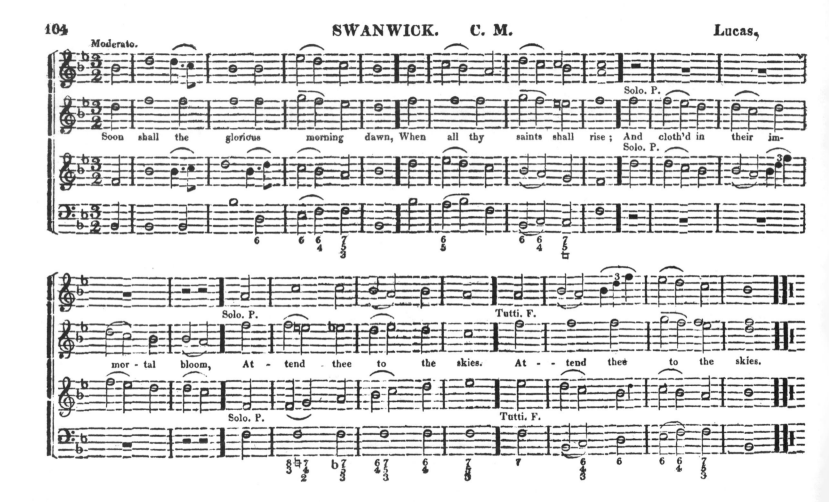

Soon shall the glorious morning dawn, When all thy saints shall rise; And cloth'd in their im-

mor - tal bloom, At - tend thee to the skies. At - tend thee to the skies.

Moderato.

How vain are all things here below! How false, and yet how fair! Each pleasure hath its poison too, And ev' - ry sweet a snare.

NOTTINGHAM. C. M.   I. Clark.

Moderato.

Some seraph lend your heav'nly tongue, Or harp of golden string, That I may raise a lofty song, To our e - ter - nal King!

CHESTERFIELD. C. M.

Dr. Haweis.

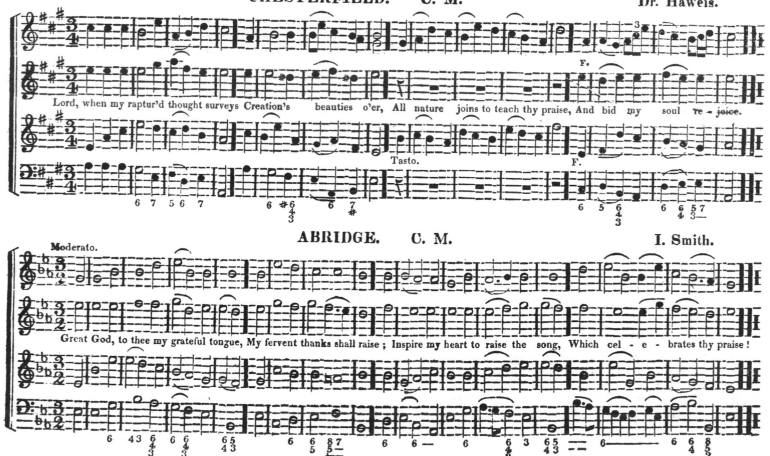

Lord, when my raptur'd thought surveys Creation's beauties o'er, All nature joins to teach thy praise, And bid my soul re - joice.

ABRIDGE. C. M.

I. Smith.

Moderato.

Great God, to thee my grateful tongue, My fervent thanks shall raise ; Inspire my heart to raise the song, Which cel - e - brates thy praise !

Cantabile.

My God, the steps of pi - ous men, Are order'd by thy will ; Though they should fall, they rise again, Thy hand sup - ports them still.

The Lord delights to see their ways, Their virtue he approves ; He'll ne'er deprive them of his grace, Nor leave the man he loves.

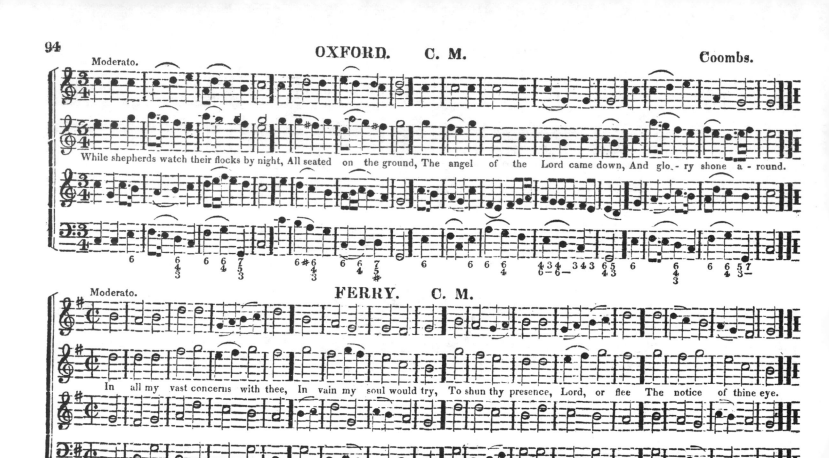

OXFORD. C. M.

Coombs.

Moderato.

While shepherds watch their flocks by night, All seated on the ground, The angel of the Lord came down, And glo-ry shone a-round.

FERRY. C. M.

Moderato.

In all my vast concerns with thee, In vain my soul would try, To shun thy presence, Lord, or flee The notice of thine eye.

TWEED. C. M.

Dr. Carter.

Sweet is the mem'ry of thy grace, My God, my heav'nly King: Let age to age thy righteousness In sounds of glo-ry sing !

PETERBOROUGH. C. M.

Once more, my soul, the rising day, Salutes my waking eyes: Once more, my voice, thy tribute pay, To him that rules the skies !

The va-rious months thy good-ness crowns: How beauteous are thy ways!

The bleat-ing flocks spread o'er the downs, And shepherds shout—And shepherds shout—And shepherds shout thy praise.

DEVIZES.   C. M.

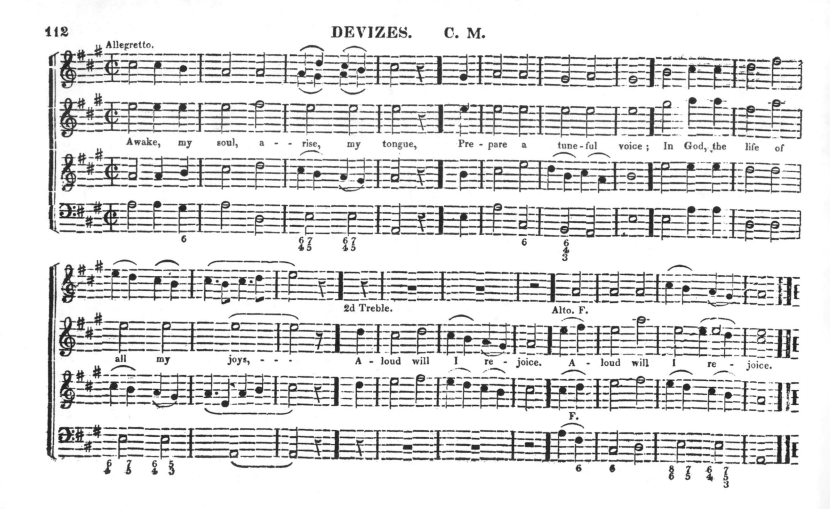

Awake, my soul, a - - rise, my tongue, Pre - pare a tune - ful voice; In God, the life of

all my joys, - - - A - loud will I re - joice. A - loud will I re - joice.

MANCHESTER. C. M.
Dr. Wainwright.

Moderato.

There is a land of liv - ing joy, Beyond the ut - most skies, Where scenes of bliss without al - loy, In boundless prospect rise.

HAMBURG. C. M.
Whitaker.

Andante é sempre piano.

Stoop down, my soul, that use to rise, Converse a while with death! Think how a gasping mortal lies, And pants away his breath!

15

CLIFFORD. C. M.

To Zion's hill I lift mine eyes, From thence is all my aid ; From Zion's hill and Zi - on's

God, From Zi - on's hill and Zi - on's God, Who heav'n and earth has made, Who heav'n and earth has made.

HULL.   C. M.

Animated.

O thou, to whom all creatures bow, Within this earthly frame, Through all the world how great art thou, How glorious is thy name?

DEDHAM.   C. M.

My Shepherd is the living Lord, No thing therefore I need; In pastures fair near pleasant streams, He setteth me to feed.

Lord, in the morning thou shalt hear My voice ascending high; To thee will I direct my pray'r, To thee lift up mine eye.

ABINGTON.   C. M.   Dr. Heighington.

Far from the world, O Lord, I flee, From strife and tumult far; From scenes where sin is waging still, Its most suc-cess-ful war.

Maestoso.

Be - - gin, my soul, the lof - ty strain, In sol - - - emn ac - cent sing,

A sacred hymn of grate - ful praise, To heav'n's Al - - migh - ty King!

IRISH. C. M.

A. Williams.

Now shall my inward joys arise, And burst in - to a song; Almighty love in-spires my heart, And pleasure tunes my tongue.

MEAR. C. M.

O, 'twas a joyful sound to hear, Our tribes de - vout - ly say, Up, Is'rael, to the tem-ple haste, And keep the festal day!

Come, let us join our cheer - ful songs, With an - gels round the throne ;

Ten thou - sand, thou - - - sand are their tongues, But all their joys are one.

LONDON.   C. M.
Dr. Croft.

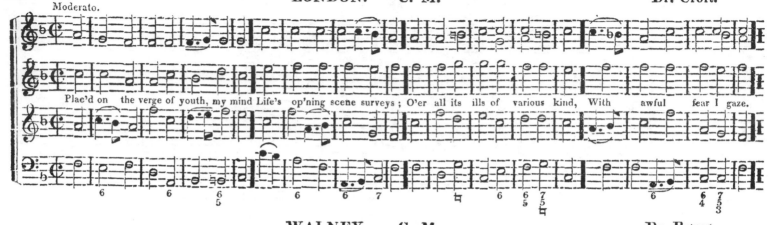

Plac'd on   the verge of youth, my mind Life's op'ning scene surveys ; O'er all its ills of   various kind, With   awful   fear I gaze.

WALNEY.   C. M.
Dr. Boyce.

Sing   to the Lord Je - ho - vah's name, And in his strength rejoice ! When his sal - va - tion   is   our theme, Ex   alt - ed   be our voice !

ARUNDEL. C. M.

All glory be to God on high, And on the earth be peace! Good will, henceforth, from heav'n to men, Begin and never cease!

ROCHESTER. C. M.

God, my sup-port-er and my hope, My help for - ev-er near; Thine arm of mercy held me up, When sinking in de-spair.

Maestoso.

CHRISTMAS. C. M.

Handel.

A - wake, my soul, stretch ev'ry nerve, And press with vigor on! A heav'n - ly

race de - mands thy zeal, And an im - mor - tal crown. And an im - mor - tal crown.

YORK. C. M.
John Milton, father of the Poet.

Thee we adore, E - ter-nal Name, And humbly own to thee, How feeble is our mortal frame, What dying worms are we!

BRADFORD.* C. M.
Handel.

* The tune Messiah, page 102, was inserted by mistake.

I know that my Re - deem-er lives, And ev - er prays for me; Sal - va - tion to his saints he gives, And life and lib - er - ty.

BRAINTREE. C. M.

In God's own house pro - nounce his praise, His grace he there re - veals:

To heav'n your joy and won - der raise, For there his glo - ry dwells.

Moderato.

Lord, thou wilt hear me when I pray, I am for-ev-er thine; I fear before thee all the day, Nor would I dare to sin.

MEDFIELD.   C. M.   Mather.

Affettuoso.

In early morn, without de-lay, O Lord, I seek thy face; My thirsty spirit faints away Without thy cheering grace.

DUNDEE. C. M.

Scottish.

Let not despair nor fell re - venge, Be to my bosom known ; O give me tears for oth - ers' woes, And patience for my own !

BARBY. C. M.

Hope looks beyond the bounds of time, When, what we now deplore, Shall rise in full im-mor - tal prime, And bloom to fade no more !

My God, how many are my fears, How fast my foes increase! Their number how it mul - ti - plies, How fa - tal to my peace!

BURFORD. C. M.   Purcell.

Dark was the night, and cold the ground, On which the Lord was laid ; His sweat like drops of blood ran down, In ag - o - ny he pray'd.

CROWLE. C. M.

Dr. Green.

Life is a span, a fleeting hour, How soon the vapour flies! Man is a tender, transient flow'r, That ev'n in blooming dies.

St. MARY's. C. M.

An ancient German melody, by Rathiel.

Lord, what is man, poor feeble man, Born of the earth at first? His life a shadow light and vain, Still hast'ning to the dust.

BANGOR. C. M.
Ravenscroft.

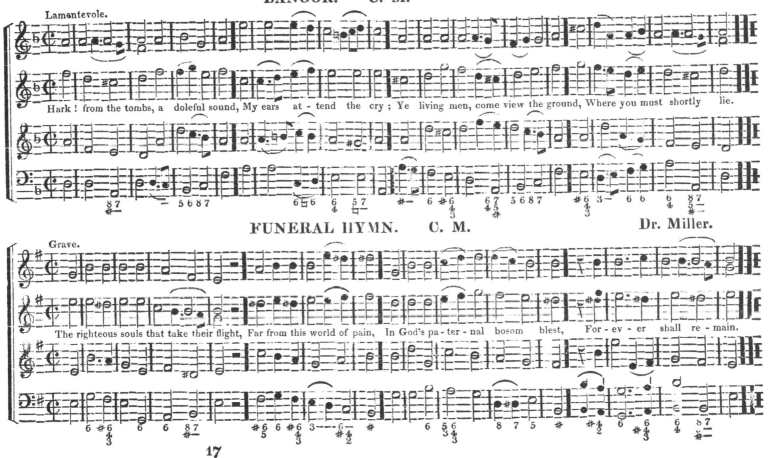

Hark! from the tombs, a doleful sound, My ears at-tend the cry; Ye living men, come view the ground, Where you must shortly lie.

FUNERAL HYMN. C. M.
Dr. Miller.

The righteous souls that take their flight, Far from this world of pain, In God's pa-ter-nal bosom blest, For-ev-er shall re-main.

17

BETHER. C. M.

Dr. Howard.

Return, O God of love, re-turn, Earth is a tiresome place; How long shall we, thy children, mourn, Our absence from thy face?

WANTAGE. C. M.

Now I forbid my carnal hope, My fond desires recall; I give my mortal int'rest up, And make my God my all.

Tenor and Alto.

Now let our droop - ing hearts re - - vive, And ev' - - ry tear be dry!

Why should these eyes be drown'd in grief, Which view a Saviour nigh?

FORELAND. C. M.

Dr. Callcott.

Thy words the rag - ing winds con - trol, And rule the boisterous deep, And rule the boisterous deep;

Thou mak'st the sleeping billows roll, - - - - - - - The rolling billows sleep, The rolling billows sleep.

JERSEY. C. M. — Dr. G. K. Jackson.

How ma-ny, Lord, of late are grown, The troublers of my peace? And as their numbers hourly rise, So does their rage in-crease.

WOOD-STREET. C. M. — Dr. G. K. Jackson.

O Lord, thou art my righteous Judge, To my complaint give ear; Thou still redeem'st me from distress, Have mercy, Lord, and hear.

WORKSOP. C. M.

To calm the sorrows of the mind, Our heav'nly Friend is nigh; To wipe the anxious tear that starts, And trembles in the eye.

HASELTON. C. M.

I. Jackson.

Help, Lord, for men of virtue fail! Re - li - gion los - es ground; The sons of wickedness pre - vail, And treacheries a - bound.

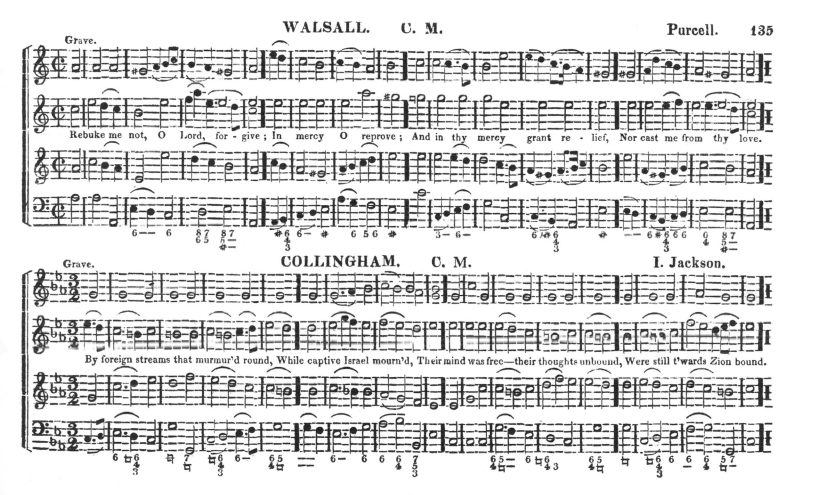

WALSALL.   C. M.   Purcell.   135

Grave.

Rebuke me not, O Lord, for-give; In mercy O reprove; And in thy mercy grant re-lief, Nor cast me from thy love.

Grave.   COLLINGHAM.   C. M.   I. Jackson.

By foreign streams that murmur'd round, While captive Israel mourn'd, Their mind was free—their thoughts unbound, Were still t'wards Zion bound.

SILVER-STREET. S. M.

I. Smith.

Come, sound his praise abroad, And hymns of glory sing! Je - ho-vah is the sov'reign God, The u - ni - ver - sal King.

Praise ye the Lord! Hallelujah! Praise ye the Lord! Hallelujah! Hallelujah! Hallelujah! Hallelujah! Praise ye the Lord!

Solo. Tutti. Unison. Solo. Tutti. Unison.

Maestoso.

My soul, re - peat his praise, Whose mercies are so great! Whose anger is so slow to rise, So ready to a - bate.

High as the heav'ns are rais'd, Above the ground we tread, So far the riches of his grace Our highest thoughts exceed, Our highest thoughts exceed.

F.

P.

F.

Unison. F.

P.

F.

18

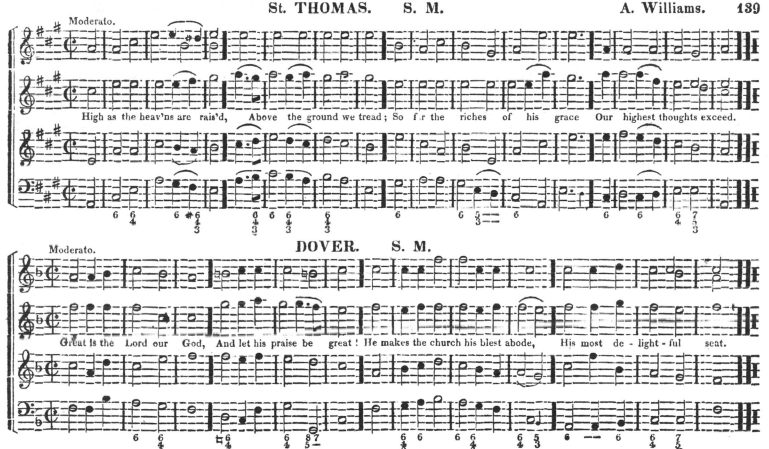

Moderato.

High as the heav'ns are rais'd, Above the ground we tread; So far the riches of his grace Our highest thoughts exceed.

DOVER.   S. M.

Moderato.

Great is the Lord our God, And let his praise be great! He makes the church his blest abode, His most de-light-ful seat.

EASTBURN. S. M.

Harwood.

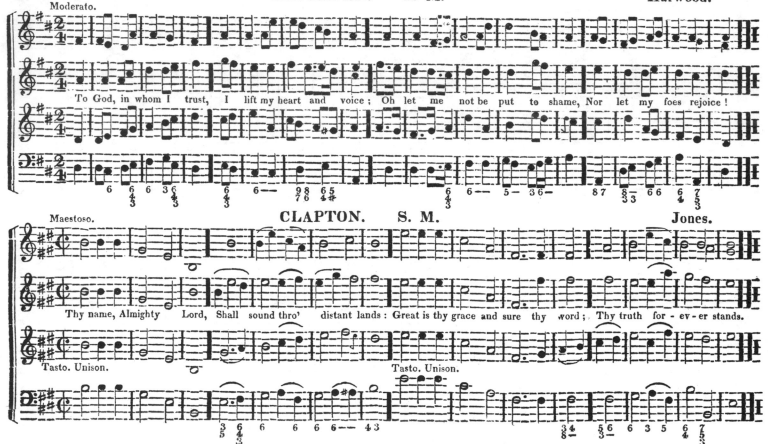

Moderato.

To God, in whom I trust, I lift my heart and voice; Oh let me not be put to shame, Nor let my foes rejoice!

6 6 6 3 6   6   6——   9 8 6 5   6 6—— 5— 3 6—   8 7 8— 6 6   6 7
   4   4   4   7 6 4 #   4 3   3 3   4 3
   3   3   3

CLAPTON. S. M.

Jones.

Maestoso.

Thy name, Almighty Lord, Shall sound thro' distant lands: Great is thy grace and sure thy word; Thy truth for- ev- er stands.

Tasto. Unison.   Tasto. Unison.

3 6   6   6 6 6—— 4 3   3 4 5 6 6 3 5 6 7
5 4   8— 3—   4 5 3
   3   3

SHIRLAND. S. M.

Stanley.

2d Treble.

Tenor.

Moderato.

Behold the morning sun, Begins his glorious way ' His beams thro' all the nations run, And life and light convey.

ATHOL. S. M.

Rev. R. Harrison.

Moderato.

How various and how new, Are thy com-pas-sions, Lord ? Each morning shall thy mercy shew, Each night thy love record.

SUTTON. S. M.

Maker and sovereign Lord, Of heav'n and earth and seas, Thy prov - i - dence confirms thy word, And answers thy decrees.

BERERIDGE. S. M.

Welcome, sweet day of rest, That saw the Lord a - rise! Welcome to this re - viv-ing breast, And these re - joic - ing eyes!

ELYSIUM. S. M.

He leads me to the hills, Where saints are blest a - bove, Where joy like morning

dew dis - tils, And all the air is love. And all the air is love.

PAISLEY. S. M. 2 verses.

Pleyel.

Andante Grazioso.

Come, we that love the Lord, And let our joys be known; Join in a song with sweet accord, And thus surround the throne!

The sorrows of the mind, Be banish'd from the place; Religion never was design'd, To make our pleasures less.

Come, Holy Spirit, come, Let thy bright beams a - rise; Dispel the darkness from our minds, And open all our eyes!

Let diff'ring nations join, To celebrate thy fame; And all the world, O Lord, com - bine, To praise thy glorious name!

19

BLANDENBURG. S. M.
German.

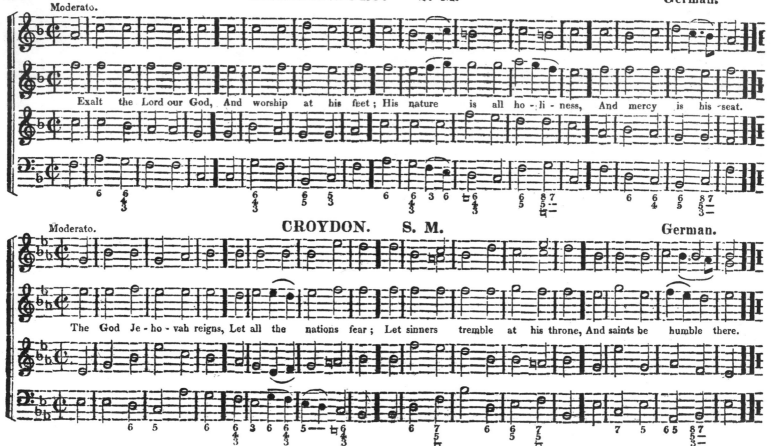

Moderato.

Exalt the Lord our God, And worship at his feet; His nature is all ho - li - ness, And mercy is his seat.

CROYDON. S. M.
German.

Moderato.

The God Je - ho - vah reigns, Let all the nations fear; Let sinners tremble at his throne, And saints be humble there.

WATCHMAN. S. M.

Leach.

Allegretto.

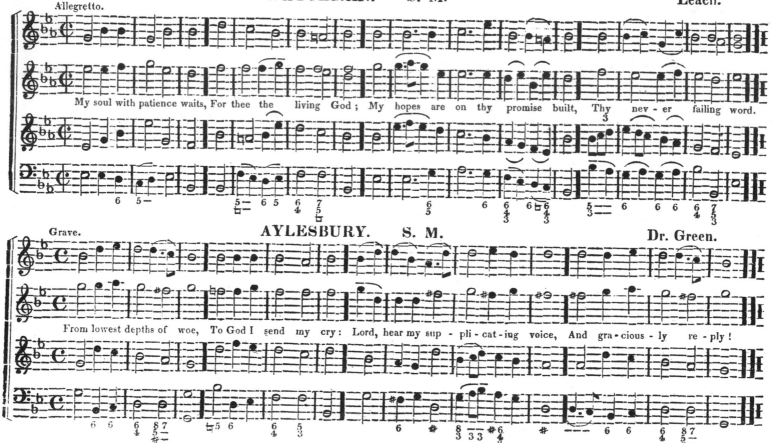

My soul with patience waits, For thee the living God ; My hopes are on thy promise built, Thy nev - er failing word.

Grave.

AYLESBURY. S. M.

Dr. Green.

From lowest depths of woe, To God I send my cry: Lord, hear my sup - pli - cat - ing voice, And gra - cious - ly re - ply!

LITTLE MARLBOROUGH. S. M.

To God, in whom I trust, I lift my heart and voice; O let me not be put to shame, Nor let my foes rejoice!

DUNBAR. S. M.

Corelli.

When overwhelm'd with grief, My heart within me dies, Helpless and far from all re - lief, To heav'n I lift my eyes.

YARMOUTH. S. M.

Wainwright.

Moderato.

Thou centre of my rest, Look down with pitying eye, While with protracted pain oppress'd, I breathe the plaintive sigh!

St. BRIDE's. S. M.

Dr. Howard.

Lamentevole.

And must this body die? This mortal frame de - cay? And must these ac - tive limbs of mine, Lie mould'ring in the clay?

Moderato.

He's blest whose sins have par - don gain'd, No more in judg - ment to ap - pear;

Whose guilt re - mis - sion has ob - tain'd, And whose re - pent - ance is sin - cere.

MARTIN's LANE. As 113th.

Dr. Arne.

I'll praise my Maker with my breath, And when my voice is lost in death, Praise shall em - ploy my nobler pow'rs.

My days of praise, shall ne'er be past, While life, and thought, and being last, Or im - mor - tal - i - ty endures.

Moderato.

Let all the earth their voices raise, To sing a lof - ty psalm of praise, And bless the great Je - ho-vah's name!

His glory let the heath - en know; His wonders to the nations show; And all his works of grace pro - claim!

20

NEWCOURT. L. P. M.

Andante.

Great God, the heav'n's well order'd frame, De-clares the glory of thy name: There thy rich works of wonder shine:

A thousand star--ry beau--ties there, A thousand ra-diant marks appear, Of boundless pow'r and skill di-vine.

The joyful morn, my God, is come, That calls me to thy honor'd dome, Thy presence to adore.

My feet the summons shall attend, With willing steps thy courts ascend, And tread the hal - low'd floor.

Be - gin, my soul, th'ex - alt - ed lay, Let each en - rap - tur'd thought o - bey, And praise th'Almighty's name!

Lo! heav'n and earth, and seas and skies, In one me - lo - dious concert rise, To swell th'in-spir-ing theme.

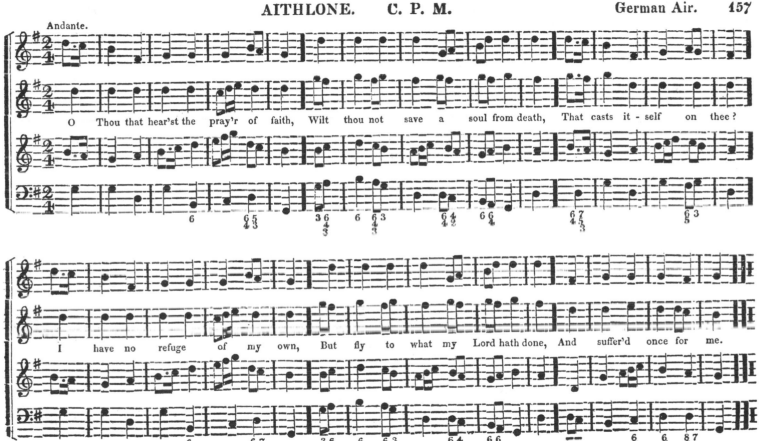

O   Thou that hear'st the pray'r of faith, Wilt thou not save a   soul from death, That casts it - self   on thee?

I   have no   refuge   of   my own, But fly to   what my Lord hath done, And   suffer'd once for me.

BIZANTIUM. C. P. M.

Dr. P. Hayes.

The Lord th'e-ter-nal sceptre rears, And nature's pow'r ob-serv-ant hears, Whate'er his will en-joins:

His head with purest splendors crown'd, With majesty he vests him round, And girds with strength his loins.

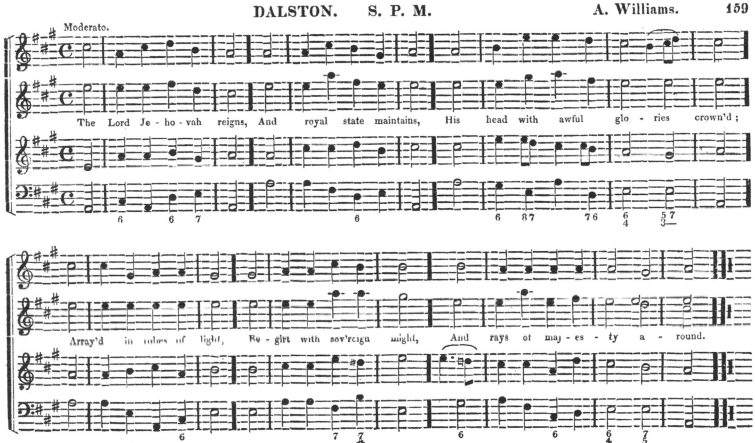

The Lord Je-ho-vah reigns, And royal state maintains, His head with awful glo-ries crown'd;

Array'd in robes of light, Be-girt with sov'reign might, And rays of maj-es-ty a-round.

WORSHIP. S. P. M.

How pleas - ant 'tis to see, Kind - red and friends a - gree, Each in their proper sta - tion move,

And each ful - fil their part, With sym - pa - thiz - ing heart, In all the cares of life and love.

Maestoso.

To God, the mighty Lord, Your joyful thanks re-peat; To him due praise af - ford, As good as

he is great. For God does prove our constant friend, His boundless love shall have no end.

21

TRIUMPH. H. M.

Lockhart.

Re - joice! the Lord is King! Your God and King adore! Mortals, give thanks and sing, And triumph

ev - er - more! Lift up your hearts, Lift up your voice! Re - joice! a - gain, I say, re - joice!

SHAFTSBURY. H. M. W. Burney.

A - wake, our drowsy souls, And burst the slothful band ; The wonders of this day, Our noblest

songs de - mand. Au - spi - cious morn, Thy bliss - ful rays, Bright seraphs hail, In songs of praise.

WEYMOUTH. H. M.

Harrison.

Jesus, our great High Priest, Hath shed his blood and died: My guil - ty conscience seeks - - - No sa - cri - fice beside.

His precious blood Di once atone, And now he pleads before the throne—His precious blood did once atone, And now he pleads before the throne.

BETHESDA. H. M.

Dr. Green.

Lord of the worlds a - bove, How pleasant and how fair, The dwellings of thy love, Thy earthly

temples are! To thine abode, My heart aspires, With warm de - sires, To see my God.

DARWELL.s.   H. M.

Rev. Mr. Darwell.

A - wake! awake! a - rise, And hail the glorious morn! Hark! how the angels sing, "To you a

Saviour's born!" Now let our hearts, In concert move, And ev'ry tongue Be tun'd to love.

Ye boundless realms of joy,   Exalt your Maker's fame, His praise your songs employ,   His praise your songs employ,   Above the starry   frame: A-

bove the starry frame. Your voices raise, Ye cherubim And seraphim, To sing his praise. Your voices raise, Ye cherubim And seraphim, To sing his praise.

MILTON. Sevens.

David Rizzio.

Moderato, a tempo Giusto.

Let us, with a joyful mind, Praise the Lord, for he is kind; For his mercies

shall en - dure, Ever faithful, ev - er sure, Ev - er faithful, ever sure.

Moderato.

Jesus, lover of my soul, Let me to thy bosom fly, While the nearer waters roll, While the tempest still is high. Hide me, O my

2d Treble. P.   Alto. F.

Saviour, hide, Till the storm of life is past, Safe into thy haven guide, O receive, O receive, O receive my soul at last.

22

PLEYEL's HYMN. Sevens.

Pleyel.

Andante é sempre piano.

Children of the heav'nly King, As ye journey sweetly sing! Sing your Saviour's worthy praise, Glorious in his works and ways!

BERNICE. Sevens.

Handel.

Andante é sempre piano.

Hark! my soul, it is the Lord, 'Tis thy Saviour, hear his word! Jesus speaks and speaks to thee, "Say, poor sinner, lov'st thou me?"

Light of life, se - raph - ic fire, Ev' - ry faint - ing soul in - spire! Love divine, thyself impart,

Shine in ev'ry drooping heart! Light of life, se - raph - ic fire, Ev'ry fainting soul inspire!

TURIN. Sevens.

Giardini.

Son of God, thy blessing grant! Still supply my ev'-ry want! Tree of life, thine influence shed,

With thy sap my spirit feed! Tree of life, thine influence shed, With thy sap my spirit feed!

NAPLES. Sevens. *Pleyel.*

Affettuoso.

Sov'reign Ruler, Lord of all, Prostrate at thy feet I fall; Hear, O hear, my ardent cry; Frown not, lest I faint and die!

PILTON. Sevens. *Weldon.*

Moderato.

Praise to God, im-mor-tal praise, For the love that crowns our days! Bounteous Source of ev'ry joy, Let thy praise our tongues employ!

ALCESTER. Sevens.

When, my Saviour, shall I be, Per-fect-ly resign'd to thee, Poor and vile in my own eyes, On-ly in thy wisdom wise?

SICILIAN HYMN. 7. or 8. 7.

Come, thou Fount of ev'ry blessing, Tune my heart to sing thy grace! Streams of mercy, never ceasing, Call for songs of loudest praise.

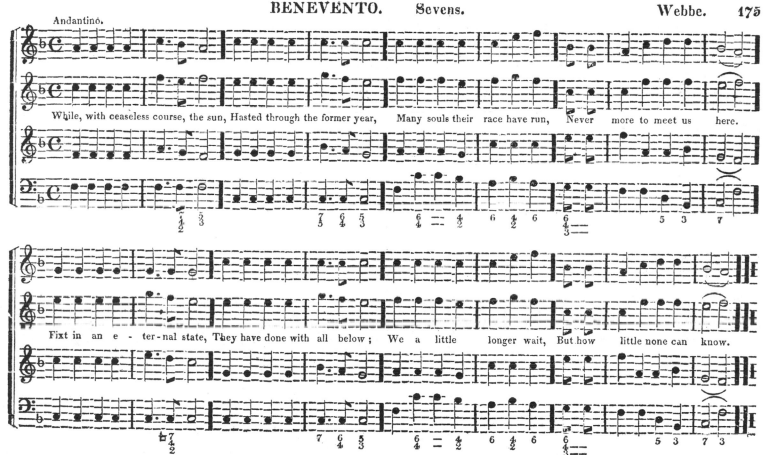

While, with ceaseless course, the sun, Hasted through the former year, Many souls their race have run, Never more to meet us here.

Fixt in an e - ter-nal state, They have done with all below; We a little longer wait, But how little none can know.

VENICE. Sevens.

Handel.

Largo.

Ho - ly Father, God of love, Look with mercy from above! Let thy streams of comfort roll,

Pia.

Let them fill and cheer my soul!

Let them fill and cheer my soul! Let them fill - - - - and cheer my soul!

Pia.

Pia.

Pia.

Let them fill and cheer my soul!

MALDEN. C. M.

Dr. G. K. Jackson.

Animated.

The heav'ns declare thy glo-ry, Lord, Which that alone can fill; The firm-a-ment and stars express, Their great Cre-a-tor's skill.

Tutti.

Ho-ly Father, God of love, Look with mercy from a-bove! Look with mercy from above!

23

SWEDEN. 7. or 8 & 7.

Clementi.

Largo con expressione.

Think, O ye who fondly languish, O'er the grave of those you love, While your bosoms throb with anguish, They are warbling hymns above !

ALSEN. 7. or 8 & 7.

F. L. Abel.

Largo.

Sov'reign Ruler of the skies, Ever gracious, ever wise, All my times are in thy hand, All events at thy command.

Larghetto con expressione.

When I tread the mortal vale, Where the shades of death prevail, Saviour guide my trembling feet, Thro' this last, this still retreat! Let thy glory chase its

gloom! Light the feeble trav'ler home! Never leave me, till I stand, Safe in yonder heav'nly land!

AUSTRIA. 7. or 8 & 7. Mozart.

Largo. Affettuoso.

O'er the hills I lift mine eyes, To those hills beyond the skies; Thence my soul her help de - rives,

There my ho — ly Re - fuge lives. There my ho — ly Re - fuge lives.

Allegretto.

High in yonder realms of light, Far above these lower skies, Fair and ex - quis - ite - ly bright, Heav'n's unfading mansions rise;

Built of pure and massy gold, Strong and du - ra - ble are they; Deck'd with gems of worth untold, Subjected to no decay.

AMBOYNA. 7. or 8 & 7.

Battishill.

Gracious Spirit, Love divine, Let thy light with-in me shine! All my guilty fears remove, Fill me full of heav'n and love!

Speak thy pard'ning grace to me, Set the burden'd sinner free! Lead me to the Lamb of God, Wash me in his precious blood!

Mighty God, E - ter - nal Father, Now we glo - ri - fy thy name; Lord of all cre - at - ed nature,

Thou art ev'ry creature's theme— Hal - le - lu - jah! Hal - le - lu - jah! Hal - le - lu - jah! A - - men!

ATHENS. 8 & 7.

Pleyel.

Andante.

Lord Almighty, gracious Father, Thou art all my hope and fear; When in danger thou in mercy, Lord, dost hear my humble pray'r.

Dolce é Sostenuto.

REUBENS. 8 & 7.

Paesiello.

1. When the winter's tempest lowers, O'er a bleak and cloudy sky, Nature's fading fruits and flowers, Hang their drooping heads and die.

2. So my bosom comforts languish, Like a lil-y over-blown, And my heart is fill'd with an-guish, When I see my Saviour frown.

Lo! he comes, with clouds de - scend - ing, Once for favour'd sin - ners slain,

Thousand, thousand saints at - tend - ing, Swell the triumph of his train.—

Hal - le - lu - jah! Hal - le - lu - jah! Hal - le - lu - jah! Je - sus now shall ever reign.

Solo.   Tutti. F.

24

ANGOLA. Sevens.

Himmel.

Rise, ye saints, to praise your King! All your sweetest passions raise, Holy pleasure while you sing, Blending with your notes of praise!

GANGES. 8. 7. or 8, 7 & 4.

Beethoven.

Praise the Lord, the great Creator, Bounteous Source of ev'ry joy: Praise him all ye works of nature: Let his praise our tongues employ!

Hark! the voice of love and mercy, Sounds a - loud from Cal - va - ry! See! it rends the rocks a - sun - der,

Shakes the earth and veils the sky! "It is finish'd!" "It is finish'd!" Hear the dying Saviour cry!

SEVILLE. 8 & 7. or 8, 7 & 4.

Woelfl.

In the floods of trib - u - la-tion, While the billows o'er me roll, Je - sus whispers con - so - la - tion,

And sup - ports my fainting soul— Sweet af - flic - tion!—Sweet af - flic - tion—That brings Je - sus to my soul!

Gently, Lord, oh! gently lead us, Thro' this lowly vale of tears; And, O Lord, in mercy give us, Thy rich grace in all our fears!

Oh! re-fresh us with thy blessing: Oh! re-fresh us with thy grace—Oh! re-fresh us—Oh! re-fresh us—Oh! re-fresh us with thy grace.

WILNA. 8. 7. or 8, 7 & 4. Monsigni.

Lord, in mer-cy, oh! pro-tect us! Keep, oh! keep us thro' the day! Thou a-lone canst on-ly save us;

Un-to Thee we sing and pray. Lord, in mer-cy, oh! pro-tect us! Keep, oh! keep us thro' the day!

Moderato.

Lord, dis - miss us   with thy blessing, Fill our hearts with   joy and peace! Let us,   each thy love pos - sess - ing,

Triumph   in re - deem - ing grace.   Oh! re - fresh us! Oh! re - fresh us, Trav'ling thro' this   wil - der - ness!

AUTUMN. 8 & 7.

Viotti.

P. Largo. Cantabile é sostenuto.

See the leaves, around us falling, Dry and wither'd to the ground! Thus to thoughtless mortals calling, In a sad and solemn round—

"Sons of Adam, (once in Eden, "When like us, he blighted fell,) "Hear the lecture we are reading, "'Tis, a - las! the truth we tell!"

Rise, my soul, stretch out thy wings, Thy better portion trace; Rise from tran - si - to - ry things, Tow'rds heav'n thy native place.

2d Treble. P. Alto. F.

Sun and moon and stars decay, Time shall soon this earth remove; Rise, my soul, and haste away, To seats prepar'd above.

TRIVOLI. 8 & 7. or 8, 7 & 4.

Pleyel.

See from Zion's sacred mountain, Streams of liv- ing water flow ! God has open'd there a fountain,

This sup - plies the plains be - low. They are blessed— They are blessed, Who its sov'reign

Blessed, Tutti. Solo. Blessed, Tutti. P. Solo.

P. Solo. Tutti. Solo. Tutti. P. Solo.

Blessed,

virtue know. They are blessed,— They are blessed, Who its sov'reign virtue know.

EASTABROOK. 8 & 7. Dr. Boyce.

Expressivo.

Weigh the words of my profession, Lord, in thine in - dul-gent scale, Of a Father's prepossession, Let my thoughts themselves avail!

Lord, not e'en an - gel - ic nature, Can sustain thy brightness near; How then can a mortal creature, Dare to meet thy eye severe?

196

TAMWORTH. 8, 7 & 4. Andante. Lockhart.

Guide me, O thou great Je-ho-vah, Pilgrim thro' this barren land!

I am weak, but thou art mighty, Hold me with thy pow'rful hand!—Bread of heaven, Bread of heaven, Feed me till I want no more!

Tasto.

Andante. TREVECCA. Sevens.

The first 8 measures are by MILGROVE, the other 8 by WHITAKER.

Jesse's son awakes the lyre: Listen while the Psalmist sings! His the Spirit's sacred fire, And his theme the King of kings.

Others sing of worldly things, Themes like these to men belong; But when Israel's Psalmist sings, Sacred themes inspire his song.

Jesse's son awakes the lyre: Listen while the Psalmist sings! His the Spirit's sacred fire, And his theme the King of kings.

WICKLOW. 8 & 7. or 8, 7 & 4. Florio.

When the vale of death ap-pears, (Faint and cold this mor-tal clay,) Kind fore-runner sooth my fears,

Light me thro' the darksome way! Light me thro' the darksome way! Break the shadows, Break the shadows,

Ush - er   in   e - ter - nal   day!

Sym.

GOSHEN.   Eights.

Moderato.

Ye angels, who stand round the throne, And view my Immanuel's face,   In rapturous songs make him known, Tune all your soft harps to his praise!

F.

F.

WANWORTH. Eights.

Harwood.

Moderato.

My gracious Redeemer I love, His praises aloud I'll proclaim, And join with the armies above, To shout his a dor-a-ble name.

SPRING. Eights.

Thos. Clark.

Grazioso.

1. The winter is over and gone: The thrush whistles sweet on the spray, The turtle breathes forth her soft moan, The lark mounts and warbles away.

2. Shall every creature around, Their voices in concert unite, And I the most favour'd be found, In praising to take less delight?

3. Awake, then, my harp and my lute! Sweet organs your notes softly swell! No longer my lips shall be mute, The Saviour's high praises to tell.

4. His love in my heart shed abroad, My graces shall bloom as the spring; This temple, his Spirit's abode, My joy, as my duty, to sing.

From Jesse's root, behold a branch a - rise,   Whose sacred flow'r with fragrance fills the skies:

The sick and weak, the healing plant shall aid,   From storms a shelter, and from heat a shade.

26

MILFIELD. Eights.

Dr. Arne.

Encompass'd with clouds of distress, Just ready all hope to resign, I pant for the light of thy face, And fear it will never be mine.

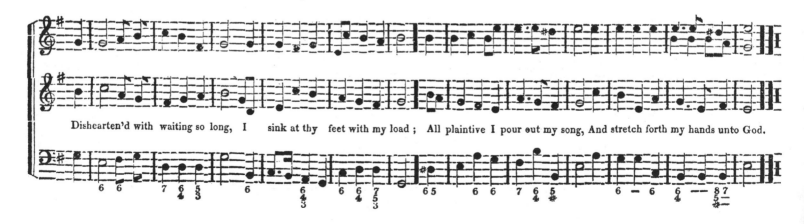

Dishearten'd with waiting so long, I sink at thy feet with my load; All plaintive I pour out my song, And stretch forth my hands unto God.

The Lord is our shepherd, our guardian, and guide: What - ev - er we want he will kindly provide. To sheep of his

pasture his mercies a - bound. His care and protection, His care and protection, His care and protection his flock will surround.

HAMILTON. 10 & 11.

The day is far spent, the ev'ning is nigh, When we must lay down the body and die.

Great God we sur - ren-der our dust to thy care ; But, oh ! for the summons our spirit prepare !

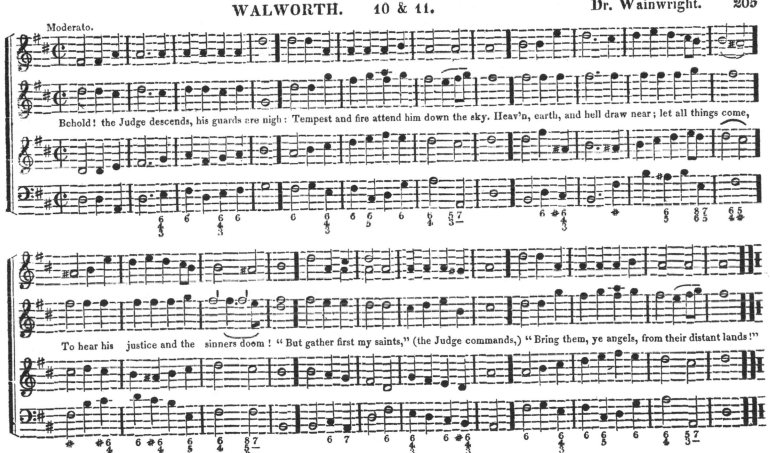

Behold! the Judge descends, his guards are nigh: Tempest and fire attend him down the sky. Heav'n, earth, and hell draw near; let all things come,

To hear his justice and the sinners doom! "But gather first my saints," (the Judge commands,) "Bring them, ye angels, from their distant lands!"

MONTAGUE. 10 & 11.

Not to our names, thou   only just and true,   Not to our worthless names is glory   due ; Thy pow'r and grace, thy truth and justice claim,

Immortal   honours to thy sov'reign name. Shine thro' the earth from heav'n thy blest abode, Nor let the heathen say, "Where is your God?"

Adagio é sempre piano.

My Father, my God, I long for thy love, Oh! shed it a - broad; send Christ from a - - bove!

My heart ever fainting he only can cheer, And all things are wanting, 'till Je - sus is here.

LYONS. 10 & 11.

Haydn.

Oh! praise ye the Lord, pre-pare a new song; And let all his saints in full concert join!

With voices u - nit - ed, the anthem pro - long, And shew forth his praises in mu - sic di - vine.

Oh! praise ye the Lord, prepare your glad voice, His praise in the great as-sem-bly to sing!

In their great Cre - a-tor let all men re-joice, And heirs of sal - va-tion be glad in their King!

27

LANDAFF. 10 & 11. E. Blancks.

The God of glory sends his summons forth, Calls the south nations and awakes the north: From east to west his sov'reign orders spread,

Thro' distant worlds and regions of the dead.—*The trumpet sounds; hell trembles, heav'n rejoices; Lift up your heads, ye saints, with cheerful voices!*

Come, saints, and a - dore him: come bow at his feet! Oh! give him the glory, the praise that is meet!

Let joyful ho - san - nas un - ceas - ing a - rise, And join the full chorus that gladdens the skies!

BERMONDSEY. 6 & 4. Milgrove.

Glory to God on high! Let earth and skies reply, Praise ye his name! His love and grace adore, Who all our sorrows bore! Sing aloud,

evermore, Worthy the Lamb!— Worthy the Lamb!— Worthy the Lamb!— Sing aloud, evermore, Worthy the Lamb!

ITALIAN HYMN. 6 & 4. Giardini. 213

Maestoso.

Come, thou Almighty King, Help us thy name to sing, Help us to praise! Father all glorious, O'er all victorious, Come and reign over us, Ancient of days!

Tasto.

NATIVITY. Sevens. Dr. G. K. Jackson.

Tenor. Dolce.

2d Treble.

P.

Treble. Hark! the skies with music sound, Heav'nly glory beams around; Christ is born, the angels sing, Glory to the new-born King!

Base.

F.

Unis.

HINTON. Elevens. German Air.

The Lord is our shepherd, our guardian, and guide: What - ev - er we want he will kind - ly provide.

To sheep of his pas - ture his mercies a - bound, His care and pro - tec - tion his flock will surround.

Maestoso.

Be - fore Je - -ho - vah's aw - ful throne, Ye na - tions bow with sa - cred joy! Know that the Lord is

God a - lone, He can cre - ate, and he de - stroy, He can cre - ate, and he de - - stroy.

216

Trio.

P. His sov'-reign pow'r, with - out our aid, Made us of clay, and form'd us men ; And when, like

wand'ring sheep, we stray'd, He brought us to his fold a - gain, He brought us to his fold a - gain.

Tutti. F.

We'll crowd thy gates with thank - ful songs, High as the heav'ns our voic - - es raise; And

Tutti. F.

6

earth, and earth with her ten thousand thousand tongues, Shall fill thy courts with sounding praise, Shall

Unison.

Unis.

28

fill thy courts with sounding praise, Shall fill, Shall fill thy courts with sound - ing praise.

Unison.

Wide! Wide as the world is thy com - mand, Vast as e - ter - ni - ty, e - ter - ni - ty thy love;

Unison.

Unison.

Firm as a rock thy truth shall stand, When roll - ing years shall cease to move, shall cease to

move, When roll -- ing years shall cease to move, When roll -- ing years shall cease to move.

SCOTLAND. Twelves. Dr. Clark.

The voice of free grace cries escape to the mountain! For all that believe Christ hath open'd a fountain, For sin, and uncleanness, and ev'-ry transgression: His blood flows so freely, in streams of salvation, His blood flows so freely, in streams of salvation.

CHORUS.

Hal - le - lu - jah! to the Lamb who has bought us a pardon! We'll praise him a - gain, when we pass over Jordon, We'll praise him a - gain, when we pass over Jordon.

DENBIGH.

Dr. Madan.

From all that dwell be - -low the skies, Let the Cre - a - tor's praise a - rise; Let the Re-

deem - er's name be sung, Thro' ev'ry land by ev' - ry tongue. E - ter - nal are thy mercies,

By ev' - ry tongue. F.

Thro' ev' - ry land by ev' - ry tongue. F.

Lord, E - ter - nal truth at - tends thy word; Thy praise shall sound from shore to shore, Till suns shall

rise and set no more, Till suns shall rise and set no more, Till suns shall rise and set no more.

THE DYING CHRISTIAN.

Harwood.

Vital spark of heav'nly flame, Quit, oh! quit this mortal frame! Trembling, hoping, ling'ring, flying;—

Oh! the pain, the bliss of dying! Cease, fond nature, cease thy strife, And let me languish into life!

Hark!

Hark!

Hark!

Hark! they whis-per, an-gels say, they whis-per, an-gels say, they whisper, they whisper, angels say—

Hark!

Hark!

Hark!

Hark!

Hark!

Hark!

P. 2d Treble.

F. Alto.

P.

"Sister spirit, come a-way!" "Sister spi-rit, come a-way!" What is this ab-sorbs me quite,

P.

F.

P.

29

226

Steals my senses, shuts my sight, Drowns my spirits, draws my breath? Tell me, my soul, can this be death?

Andantino.

Tell me, my soul, can this be death! The world re-cedes, it dis-ap-pears; Heav'n o-pens

O grave, where is thy vic-to-ry, O death, where is thy sting? Lend, lend your wings! I mount, I fly, O

6 3 6 3 ——— Unison.   5 3 ——   6 — 5
      4   4   4   3
      3   2

grave, where is thy victory? thy victory? O grave, where is thy victory? thy victory? O death, where is thy sting, O death, O

6 — 5 6 3 — 5 — 3 ——   6 — 5 —6 3 — 5 — 3 ——   6 — 3 ——
4   3   4   3

death, where is thy sting? Lend, lend your wings! I mount, - - - I fly, O grave, where is thy

vic - to - ry? thy vic - to - ry? O death, O death, where is thy sting?

CHESHUNT.

Dr. Arnold.

Maestoso.

Our Lord is risen from the dead, Our Jesus is gone up on high ; The pow'rs of hell are captive led, Dragg'd to the

portals of the sky, The pow'rs of hell are captive led, Dragg'd to the portals of the sky, Dragg'd to the portals of the sky.

There his triumphal chariot waits, And an-gels chant the sol-emn lay; "Lift up your heads, ye heav'nly gates, Ye

Unison.

ev-er-last-ing doors give way! Lift up your heads, ye heav'nly gates, Ye ev-er-last-ing doors give way!

Solo.

Loose all your bars of massy light, And wide un - fold th' ethere - al scene! He claims these mansions as his right; Receive the King of

Solo.

glo - ry in! He claims these mansions as his right, Receive the King of glo - ry in! Receive the King of glo - ry in!

Loose all your bars of massy light, And wide unfold th'e - the - real scene ! He claims these mansions as his right ; Receive the King of

glo - ry in ! He claims these mansions as his right, Re - ceive the King of glo - ry in ! Re - ceive the King of glo - ry in !

30

"Who is the King of glory? who? Who, who is the King of glory? who?" "The Lord that all our foes o'ercame, The world, sin,

death, and hell o'erthrew; And Jesus is the Conq'rors name, And Je - sus is the Conq'rors name, And Je - sus is the Conq'rors name.

Lo! his triumphal chariot waits, And an-gels chant the solemn lay, " Lift up your heads, ye heav'nly gates, Ye

Unison.

ev - er-last-ing doors give way! Lift up your heads, ye heav'nly gates, Ye ev - er-last - ing doors give way!"

"Who is the King of glory? who? who? Who? who is the King of glory?

Unison.

who?" "The Lord, of boundless pow'r pos - sess'd, The King of saints and an - gels too, God over

all, for - ev - er blest ; God o - ver all, for - ev - er blest. God o - ver all, for - ev - er

7   5   6   5   5   6   4 3
                                              5—

Adagio.

blest.   God   o - ver   all,   for - ev - er   blest— for - ev - er   blest.

5   6   6   6   5—   5   6   5—
                           4 3   4 3

THE LAST DAY.

Whitaker.

That day of wrath, that dread - ful day, When heav'n and earth shall pass a - way,

When heav'n and earth shall pass away, What pow'r shall be the sin - ner's stay? How shall he meet that

Allegretto.

dreadful day, When, shriv'ling like a parched scroll, The flam - ing heav'ns to-geth - er

roll, - - - - - to-geth-er roll— The flam - - ing heav'ns to-geth-er roll— The flaming heav'ns to-

geth-er roll—to-geth - er roll—to-geth-er roll; When louder yet, and yet more dread, Swells the high trump-

The

6 6 6 6 5 7 7
4 4 3 3 #

The

heav'ns, the heav'ns, the heav'ns together roll; The heav'ns, the heav'ns, the heav'ns together roll;

Swell the high trump,

Trumpet.

heav'ns, the heav'ns, the heav'ns together roll; The heav'ns, the heav'ns, the heav'ns together roll;

6
5

242

sinners stay, Though heav'n and earth shall pass away! Though heav'n and earth shall pass a - way! Be thou the trembling

sinners stay, Though heav'n and earth shall pass away! Though heav'n and earth shall pass a - way!

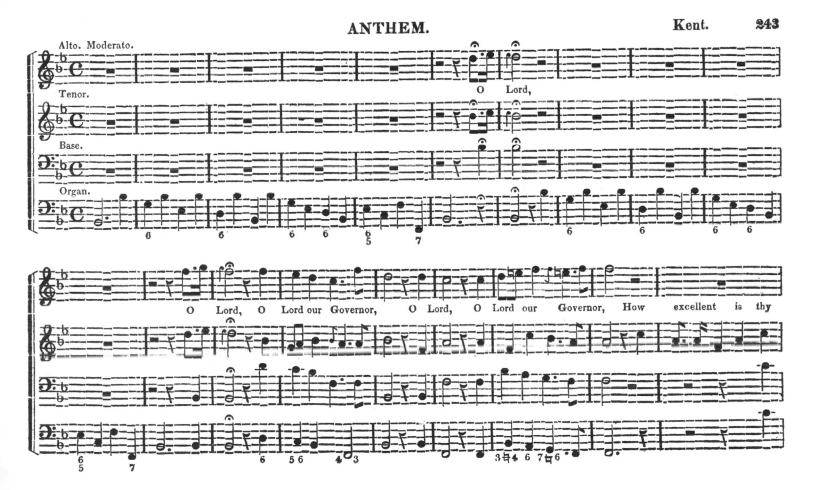

name! How excellent is thy name! How excellent! How excellent! How excellent is thy name in all the world.

How excellent! How excellent! How excellent! &c.

excellent is thy name! How excellent! How excellent! How excellent! How excellent, &c.

Thou that hast set thy glory, thy glo — — — — — — ry, thy glo — — — — — ry, hast set thy glory, thou

Duet. . Trebles.

Organ.

First Treble.

Out of the mouth of ve - - ry babes and sucklings, hast thou or - dain - ed strength, be - cause of thine

2d Treble.

enemies. Out of the mouth of ve - - ry babes and sucklings, hast thou or - dain - - ed strength, be-

cause of thine en - e - mies. *Sym.*

1st Treble.

Out of the mouth of ve - - ry babes, of ve - ry babes and sucklings, hast thou or - dain - ed, or - dain - ed

2d Treble.

strength, be - cause of thine en - e - mies, that thou might'st still the en - e - my, that thou might'st still the en - e - my,

P.

F.

P.

F.

Sym.

might'st still the en - e - my, that thou might'st still the en - e - my, might'st still the en - e - my, and

the a - veng - er, that thou might'st still the ene - my, and the avenger, that thou might'st still the enemy, and -- the a-

a - veng-er, that thou might'st still --- the en - e - my, that thou might'st still the

veng - er, that thou might'st still - - - the en - e - my, that thou might'st still the en-e-my, and - - - the avenger.

that thou might'st still the enemy and the avenger, that thou might'st still the en - e - my, and the avenger.

Recit. Tenor.

What is man, that thou art mindful of him? and the son of man, that thou vis - it - est him?

Recit. Base.

Thou madest him lower than the angels, to crown him with glory, with glo - - - - - - ry, with glo - - - - - - ry, with glory and worship.

32

CHORUS.

Verse. Treble and Base.

Let us come be - fore his presence, let us come be - fore his presence with thanks - giv - ing, with thanks-

Let us

giving ; come before his presence, let us come before his presence with thanksgiving ;

And shew ourselves glad, and shew ourselves glad, and shew ourselves glad - -

And shew ourselves glad, and shew ourselves glad, and shew our - selves

in him with psalms.

glad

CHORUS. Largo Expressivo.

For the Lord is a great God; the Lord is a great God, and a great King above all gods; a great King above all gods.

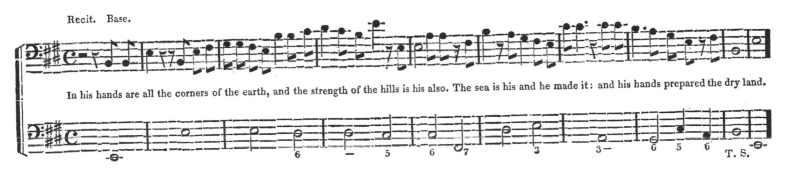

Recit. Base.

In his hands are all the corners of the earth, and the strength of the hills is his also. The sea is his and he made it: and his hands prepared the dry land.

Duet.

O come, let us worship, O come, let us worship, and fall down, and kneel be - fore the Lord, the Lord our maker.

Inst. Base.

CHORUS.

O come, let us worship; O come, let us worship, and fall down, and kneel be - fore the Lord, the Lord our maker.

Voice.

Duet.

For he is the Lord, the Lord our God ; and we are the people, we are the people, we are the people of his pasture, and the sheep of his hand.

Inst. Base.

T. S.

CHORUS.

For he is the Lord, the Lord our God!   we are the

And we are the people,

T. S.   Inst.   6

Adagio.

people,   we are the people of his pasture, and the sheep of his hand.

7   Voice.   7   6   5   6   6   6 7   5   5 7
                                        4   4 5   4   3

33

ANTHEM.

Rev. Mr. Mason.

Maestoso. Chorus.

Lord of all pow'r and might, Lord of all pow'r and might,

Solo. P.

Thou that art the author, Thou that art the author, Thou that art the giver of all good things;

Solo. P.

Solo. P.

FROM THE ORATORIO OF JUDAH.

Gardiner.

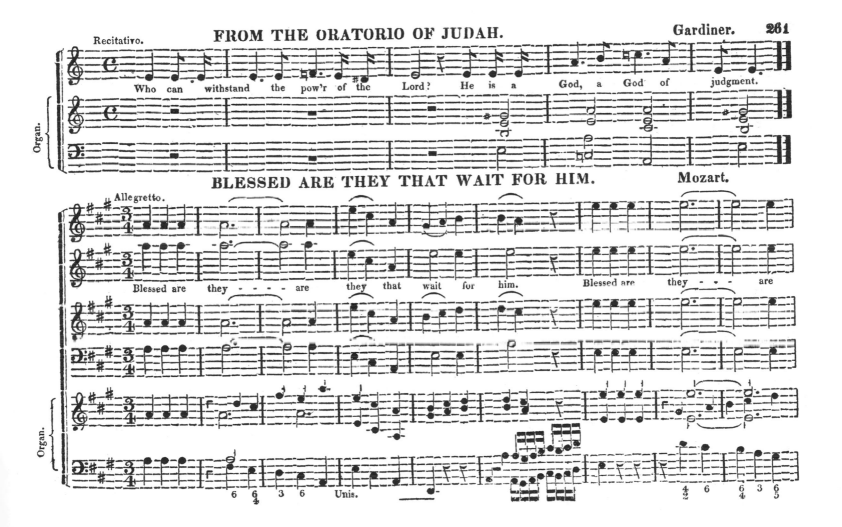

Recitativo.

Who can withstand the pow'r of the Lord? He is a God, a God of judgment.

Organ.

BLESSED ARE THEY THAT WAIT FOR HIM.

Mozart.

Allegretto.

Blessed are they - - - - are they that wait for him. Blessed are they - - - are

Organ.

6 6 3 6 Unis.   4 6 6 3 6
   4   2   4 5

they that wait for him, they shall find de - light in him, For they shall

For they shall

For

For

they shall find de - light in him, de - light, - - - - - - - de - light in him.

find de - light in him, they shall find de - light, de - light in him.

find de - light in him, de - light - - - in him, shall find de - light in him.

they shall find de - light in him, de - light, - - - - - - - - de - light in him.

For they shall find de - light - - - - - - - - - - - -

For they shall find de - light - - - - - - - - - - - -

For they shall find de - light in him, For they shall find

For they shall find de - light - - - - - - - - - - - -

in him, de - - light in him.

in him, de - - light in him, For they shall find de-

- - - de - light in him, de - - light in him.

in him, de - - light in him.

de - light in him,

- - - light - - - - in him, Blessed are they that wait for him, For

de - light in him, Blessed are they that wait for him, For

F.

For they shall find de - light in him, delight - - - - - - - - - - -

they shall find delight in him, they shall find de - light - - - -

they shall find de - light in him, de - - - - - - - - - - - - - - -

For they shall find de - light in him, delight - - - - - - - - - -

light . . . . in him, de - - - light

light, ... de - - light in him, de - - - light

him, for they shall find . . . . . . de - - light in him, de - - - light

light . . . . in him, de - - - light

FUGE. Moderato.

Let Zion and her sons re - joice, Behold the promis'd hour;

Let Zion and her sons re - joice, Her God hath

Let Zi - on and her sons re - joice, Be hold the promis'd hour; Her God hath heard her

Let Zion and her sons, her sons re - joice, Behold the promis'd hour, the promis'd hour;

6 43 0 — 6 3 7 6 6 5 4 3 0 5 — 6 5 6 — 7 7

Her God hath heard her mourning voice, Her God hath heard her mourning voice,

heard, hath heard her mourning voice, And will ex - alt his pow'r, And will exalt his pow'r, And will exalt his pow'r.

mourning voice, Her God hath heard her mourning voice,

Her God hath heard her mourning voice, her mourning voice,

5 ———— 6 ♭7 3 — 5 6 3 6 6 5♯6 4 3   6 6 6 5 6   6 7
                                                            4

ANTHEM. Suitable for Funeral occasions.

Rev. Dr. Blake.

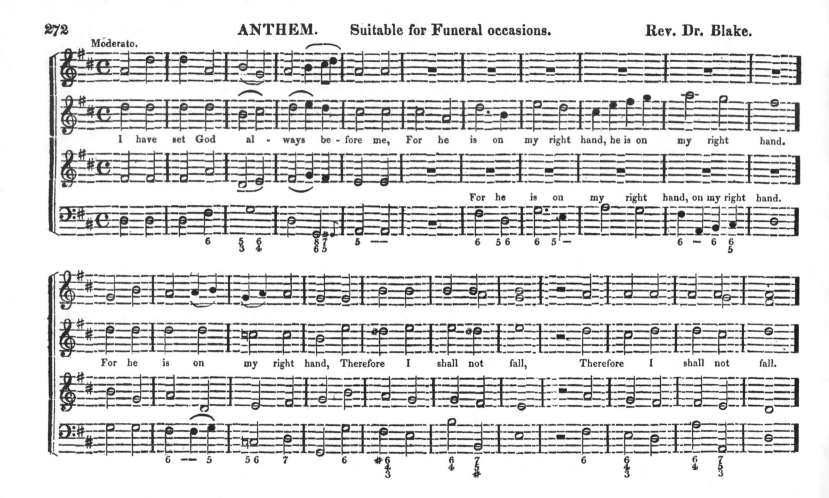

I have set God al - ways be - fore me, For he is on my right hand, he is on my right hand.

For he is on my right hand, on my right hand.

For he is on my right hand, Therefore I shall not fall, Therefore I shall not fall.

For he is on my right hand,

I have set God always, al - ways before me, For he is on my right

I have set God always before me,

I have set God al - ways before me, For he is on my right hand, on my right

therefore I shall not, i shall not fall.

hand, therefore I shall not fall. He is on my right hand, on my right hand, therefore I shall not fall.

hand, &c.

35

Andante. Trio. Two Trebles and Basé.

DUET. Andante. Two Trebles.

2d Treble.

1st Treble.

Thou shalt shew me the path of life; in thy presence is fulness of joy:

Organ.

Thou wilt shew me the path of life, in thy presence is

in - - thy presence is fulness of joy.

fulness of joy, In thy presence, thy presence is fulness of joy.

Thou shalt

6 #6 6 6 5 6 5 3 6 6 5
   4   4 3
   3

Thou shalt shew me the path of life, shalt shew me the path, the path of life.

shew me the path, the path of life. shalt shew me the path of life.

8 7 6 5 6 7 6 6 6 7 6 5 7 6 9
6 5 4 3 4 5 4 3 4 5 4 3 5 8

ev - er, for - ev - er more, plea - - - - - - - - - - - - - - - - sure, pleasure,

plea - - - - - - - - - - - - - - - - - sure, pleasure,

there is plea - sure, is plea - sure for - ev - er - more, is pleasure, is pleasure for - ev - er - more.

CHORUS.

Thou shalt shew me the path of life, in thy presence is fulness of joy.

shalt shew me, shalt shew me the path of life.

Thou shalt shew me the path of life, shalt shew me the path of life.

shalt shew me the path, the path of life.

And   at   thy   right   hand   there   is

In   thy   presence, thy   presence   is   fulness   of   joy,   And

And   at   thy   right   hand,   at

pleasure,   is   pleasure,   there   is   pleasure,

at   thy   right   hand   there   is   pleasure,   And   at   thy   right   hand there is   pleasure.

thy   right   hand   there   is   pleasure,

at thy right hand there is   pleasure,   there is   plea-sure, is   plea-sure for - ev - er - more,   is

plea - sure for - - ev - er - - more,   there is   plea-sure   for - - ev - er - more.

Adagio.

THANKSGIVING ANTHEM.

Kent.

Allegretto.

F. O — be joy - ful, O be joy - ful in the Lord, all ye lands.

F. O — be joy - ful, O be joy - ful in the Lord, all ye lands.

F. O — be joy - ful, O be joy - ful in the Lord, all — ye lands

6   7 #6   4 3

Second Treble.

Be joy — — — — — — ful,

Alto.

Be joy — — — — — — — ful,

O be joyful in

Be joy — — — — — — — — ful,

T. S.

DUET. Trebles. Andante.

Be ye sure that the Lord he is God, it is he, it is he that hath made us, and not we our-

ORGAN.

selves, We are his people, We are his people, and the sheep of his pasture.

ra - tion, from gen - e - - ra - tion, from gen - e - ration to gen - e - - ration.

ra - tion to gene - - - - - - - ra - - - - - - - tion, from gen - e - ration to gen - e - - ration.

ra - tion, from gene - - ra - - - - - - tion, from gen - e - ration to gen - e - - ration.

Chorus. Allegretto.

Glory   be to the   Father,   and   to the   Son,   and   to the   Ho - ly   Ghost:

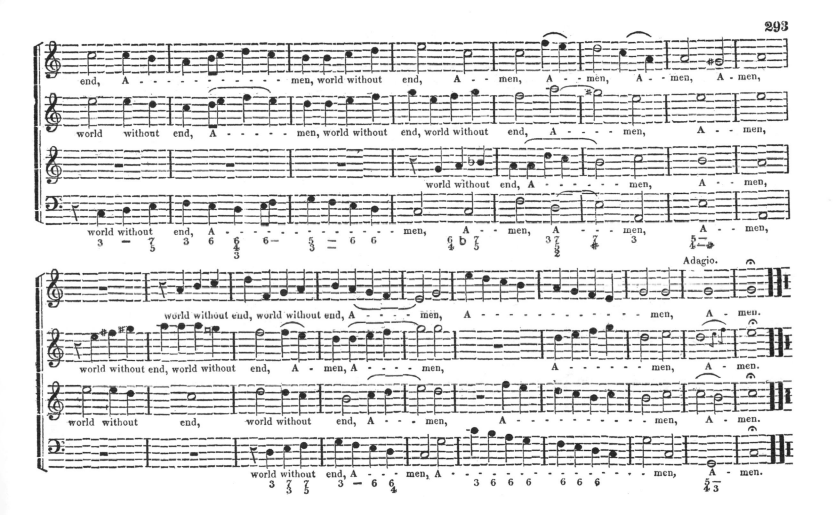

THE LORD'S PRAYER.

Denman.

Our Father, who art in heav'n, hal-low-ed be thy name, Thy kingdom come, thy will be done, on

Our Father, who art in heav'n, hal-low-ed be thy name, Thy kingdom come, thy will be done, on

earth as it is in heav'n; Give us this day our dai - ly bread, and for - give us our tres-pass - es, as

earth as it is in heav'n; Give us this day our dai - ly bread, and for - give us our tres-pass - es, as

we for-give them that tres-pass a-gainst us, and lead us not in-to temp-ta-tion, but de-liv-er us from

we for-give them that tres-pass a-gainst us, and lead us not in-to temp-ta-tion, but de-liv-er us from

38

e - vil, for thine is the kingdom, and the pow - er, and the glo - ry, for ev - er, and ev - er,

e - vil, for thine is the kingdom, and the pow - er, and the glo - ry, for ev - er, and ev - er,

ANTHEM.

Kent.

Blessed, blessed be thou, Lord God of Is - ra - el, our Fa - ther, Blessed, blessed be thou, Lord

God of Is - ra - el, our Father, for ev - er and ev - er, for ev - er and ev - er, blessed, blessed be thou, Lord

Bless - - - ed, bless - - - ed,

T. S. - - - - - - - - - - - - -

Bless - ed, for ev - er,

Bless - ed, Blessed art thou, for ev - er and ev - er, for ever and ever.

for ev - er and ev - er,

for ev - er, for ev - er, and ev - er, for ev - er,

Two voices.

Thine, O Lord, O Lord, is the greatness. Thine, O Lord, O Lord, is the greatness.

Organ.

greatness and the pow'r, is the greatness and the pow'r, and the glory, and the victory, and the majesty, the majesty, for all that

Organ.   Voice.   Organ.   Voice.

is in the heav'n, in the heav'n and the earth are thine: Thine is the kingdom, thine is the kingdom, O

For all that is in the heav'n,

Organ.   Voice.

Lord, and thou art ex - alted as head over all, as head over all, as head, as head over all.

over all,

as head over all.

DUET.

Both riches and hon - our come of thee, come of thee, riches and honour come of thee,

39

And thou reignest, thou reignest, thou reignest over all; and in thine hand, in thine hand is

is pow'r,

T. S.

And in thine hand it is to make great, and to give strength un - to all.

pow'r and might, and in thine hand it is to make great, to make great, and to give strength un - to all.

prai - - - - - - - - se thy glorious name, we thank thee, and praise thy glorious

name, we thank thee, and prai - - - - se thy glorious

thank thee, and praise thy glorious

thank thee, we thank thee, and prai - - - - - se thy glorious name, and prai - - - - se thy

Slow.

name, thy glorious name, we thank thee, we thank thee, O God, we thank thee, we thank thee, O God, and praise thy glorious name.

PONDER MY WORDS. An Anthem for three voices. Dr. G. K. Jackson.

O PRAISE THE LORD. Canon, four in two. Wm. Horsley.

☞ *It has been thought advisable in two or three instances, to make use of the Alto and Tenor Clefs.*

name, let us mag - ni - fy his name - - - - - to - - geth - er, Let us mag-ni-fy his

me, - - - - - praise the Lord with me,

geth - er, let us mag-ni-fy his name to - geth-er, let us mag-ni-fy his name, his

praise the Lord with me, praise the Lord, - - - - - - - - - -

name to - - geth - er, let us mag - ni - fy his name, his name to - geth - er.

praise the Lord, - - - - - - - - - - - - - - - - -

name to - - geth - er, And let us mag-ni-fy his name, let us

O praise the Lord, praise the Lord with me.

O LORD MY GOD.   Canon, three in one.   Wm. Horsley.

Alto. Cheerfully.

Tenor. F. O Lord my God, I will ex - alt, - - - - - - - - - I will ex - alt - - - - - -

F. O Lord my God, I will ex - alt - - - - -

F. O

- - - thee, and I will praise thy name, will praise thy name for - - ev - er, and

- - - - I will ex - alt - - - - - thee, and I will praise thy name, will praise thy

Lord my God, I will ex - alt, - - - - - - I will ex - alt - - - - - - - thee, and

ever, for - ever and ever, I will praise thy name, will praise thy name, thy name

name for - ever and ever, for - ever and ever, I will praise thy name, will praise thy

I will praise thy name, will praise thy name for - ever and ever, for - ever and

for ev - er, O Lord my God, I will ex - alt, - - - - - - I will ex - alt - - - - -

name, thy name, for - - ev - er, O Lord my God, I will ex - alt - - - - - -

ever, I will praise thy name, will praise thy name, thy name for - - - ever, O

O 'TWAS A JOYFUL SOUND.

Canon for three voices.

Dr. G. K. Jackson.

courts we must, we must ap - pear with our assem - bled pow'r, In strong and

at Salem's courts we must, we must ap - pear with our assembled pow'r.

day, at Sa - lem's courts we must, we must ap - pear with our assembled

Finis. :S:

beauteous order rang'd like her u - ni - ted tow'rs. O 'twas, &c.

Finis. :S:

In strong and beauteous order rang'd like her u - ni - ted tow'rs. O 'twas, &c.

Finis. :S:

pow'r, In strong and beauteous order rang'd like her u - ni - ted tow'rs.

N. B. To be sung twice from the repeat, :S; and end at the pause, ⌒.

CANON. **Three in one.** Dr. G. K. Jackson.

Hear my pray'r, O Lord, and give ear unto my call-ing, O my God. Hear my prayer, O Lord, O

Hear my prayer, O Lord, and give ear unto my calling, O my God, Hear my prayer, O

Hear my prayer, O Lord, and give ear unto my calling, O my God. Hear my

Lord, when I mourn, when I mourn, when I mourn, O my God, hear my prayer, O Lord, and give

Lord, O Lord, when I mourn, when I mourn, when I mourn, O my God, Hear my prayer, O

prayer, O Lord, O - - Lord, when I mourn, when I mourn, when I mourn, O my God. Hear my

N. B. **To be sung twice from the repeat, :S: and end at the pause,**

ALPHABETICAL INDEX.

41

ALPHABETICAL INDEX *Continued.*

METRICAL INDEX.

METRICAL INDEX *Continued.*